QLIK SENSE
FOR
BEGINNERS

GW00481170

By

MARK O'DONOVAN

www.techstuffybooks.com

Disclaimer

Although the author and publisher have made every effort to ensure that the information in this book was correct at press time, the author and publisher do not assume and hereby disclaim any liability to any party for any loss, damage, or disruption caused by errors or omissions, whether such errors or omissions result from negligence, accident, or any other cause.

Information sold in this book is sold without warranty, either expressed or implied.

Title: Qlik Sense For Beginners

Version: 1.1

Published by TechStuffy Books

CONTENTS

PART 1

TEACH ME QLIK SENSE

WHO IS THIS BOOK AIMED AT

Anyone who currently uses a spreadsheet, text file or database to save information and thinks it might be useful to analyze this information.

This could be the everyday person who wants to track their personal finances or how they are progressing in their exercise\weight loss program.

This could be the IT user who wants to explore SQL backup data, web server logs or SQL server reporting services (SSRS) logs.

This could be the finance person who wants to use Qlik Sense to explore Revenue Information or Invoice Details.

Some reasons to use Qlik Sense after you learn the basics from this book and tried some examples:

- It makes it easier to explore data and make decisions.
- It is helping you with your goals in life such as budgeting.
- You are using it at work whether in IT, Finance or another department.
- You might find that it helps you save you money.
- You see it more and more in job advertisements and feel it is something you should learn.

The main reason to use Qlik Sense is that you think it is a useful tool.

WHY LEARN QLIK SENSE AND NOT QLIKVIEW

QlikView is a great product and you might be wondering why you should learn Qlik Sense.

Here are a few reasons why I think it is worth spending your time learning Qlik Sense:

- You like some of the features such as Storytelling that are in Qlik Sense but not in QlikView.

- You find the responsive design of Qlik Sense that rearranges objects such as tables\charts depending on the size of the screen very useful.

- You are an IT freelancer\contractor and want to stay ahead of the game and be prepared for any opportunities that come when companies need someone with Qlik Sense experience to help migrate their QlikView applications.

- At some point it the future Qlik will drop support for QlikView so it is best to be prepared. Although the line from Qlik is that is that they have a dual product strategy the emphasis is most definitely on the Qlik Sense product.

Qlik Sense is aimed more at a self-service style of business intelligence where users are encouraged to create their own charts \ tables where they do not already exist.

Whereas QlikView which is described as 'guided analytics' generally involved more input from IT to make changes when used within a work environment.

QlikView users had the ability to create their own charts and tables but in my experience most do not do more than creating a listbox.

HOW TO USE THIS BOOK

I think the best way to use this book is to work your way through the chapters in order, then you can start creating your own Qlik Sense apps with more confidence.

If you have used QlikView before you might be familiar with the scripts used in the data load editor (loadscripts in QlikView).

In this case you might be tempted to skip parts of chapters but this might just cause more confusion later on if your apps don't resemble the screenshots in the book.

The completed applications with be included with the sample data.

These completed apps are useful to see what you will achieve through using this book and later to compare against your own apps.

The sample data and completed apps are FREE to download whether or not you have purchased the book.

Any references in this book to Qlik Sense refer to the Qlik Sense Desktop application that is free to download from qlik.com.

EXAMPLES IN THIS BOOK

You can download all the sample data for this book from:

http://www.techstuffy.com/downloads

The sample data will be in a zip file containing all the data used for the examples (QS4B Data Sources) within the book as well as solutions to the examples (QS4B Sample files).

The data for the AdventureWorks Access Database is a separate download.

EXAMPLE APPS

Throughout the book there will referenced to the 'completed app' in the sample data, these apps are to help you if you get stuck with the examples.

Also some apps are referred to as 'starting app', these apps are just to provide a starting point for the example.

The data sources for these apps were loaded from the folder:

C:\QLIK SENSE SAMPLE DATA\data sources

If you are using these apps and your data sources (such as Excel and text files) are in a different location you will need to update the connection in the data load editor.

To edit the connection go the Data Load Editor (DLE) and click the pencil icon for the 'data sources' folder and change the folder path, move the cursor to the folder name and click save.

You will learn more about the Data Load Editor as you

work your way through the book.

USING EXAMPLE APPS

To add the solutions to your hub, copy the qvf files to the following folder:

C:\Users\<yourusername>\Documents\Qlik\Sense\Apps

The press F5 to refresh the hub and the application should appear.

You will learn more about moving apps between computers within the book.

ABOUT THE AUTHOR - MARK O'DONOVAN

Mark O'Donovan has been working within the IT industry for over 18 years within IT support and developer roles.

For over 6 years Mark has been focused on SQL Server development and business intelligence applications such as Microsoft BI and QlikView.

Mark is currently working as a QlikView developer in London.

WEBSITES

To keep up-to-date with QlikView\Qlik Sense by subscribing to one of the following sites:

http://www.techstuffy.com

http://twitter.com/practicalqlik

http://youtube.com/practicalqlik

OTHER PUBLICATIONS

Practical QlikView

Learn QlikView Development with lots of Practical Examples.

Practical QlikView 2 - Beyond Basic QlikView

More advanced QlikView development techniques

Practical SQL

Learn SQL Server Development from the basics o more advanced concepts.

For more information on the books search for these titles on Amazon or go to **www.techstuffybooks.com**.

AN OVERVIEW OF THIS BOOK

This book is split into various parts.

The aim of this book is to guide you from being a qlik sense beginner to someone who is ready to tackle some of the more advanced features of qlik sense development.

Next we will give you an overview of what topics will be covered in the main parts of this book:

TEACH ME QLIK SENSE

We start by explaining what Qlik Sense is and how to download and install the Qlik Sense Desktop software.

Next we cover how to create your first qlik sense app. Finally we cover some basic concepts and how to start using the Qlik Sense Desktop.

CREATING QLIK SENSE APPS

In this chapter we will describe:

- The types of files you can read data into your Qlik Sense app.

- Demonstrate example apps using Excel and Text files.

- How you can filter the data in your data model using inner joins.

Manage Data

In this chapter of the book we will focus on the data that is being brought into your Qlik Sense app.

We will cover:

- Reading data from ODBC and OLE DB connections.
- Managing the data such as creating links between 2 tables or reading less data using the WHERE clause.
- Creating expressions to calculate fields and also some useful expressions to know when loading data into your app.
- Some useful functions such as concat and count.
- Using Folder connections to create shortcuts to your data source folder contains files such as Excel and text files.

Charts and Tables

In this part of the book we will be covering:

- Bar chart
- Line chart
- Pie chart
- Tables
- Chart Expression and Groups

Development Tips

- In this part we will introduce some tips to help with your Qlik Sense development including:
- How to migrate documents from QlikView to Qlik Sense.
- How to work on apps located in other folders

rather than the default Apps folder.

- How to change the app image displayed on the desktop hub
- Finally we will cover some useful design tips when creating your Qlik Sense apps.

Advanced Topics

In this final part we will cover some of the more advanced topics such as:

- Advanced sheet objects including gauges, scatter plot and treemap.
- Managing the data model.
- Calendar tables.
- Advanced functions including class, aggr, intervalmatch and dual.
- Using SQL stored procedures.
- Set analysis.
- QVDs to store data read from data sources and incremental loads.
- An introduction to qlik sense extensions.

GETTING STARTED

OVERVIEW

In this chapter we will cover:

- An introduction to QlikTech the developers of Qlik Sense.

- How to download and install Qlik Sense.

TELL ME SOMETHING ABOUT QLIK SENSE

What is this book about?

This book is a practical introduction to Qlik Sense.

First we will look at the basic concepts used in Qlik Sense so you can start using the software quickly, then we will explore different examples where Qlik Sense might be used.

If you have used QlikView before you will be familiar with the scripting techniques used to bring data into the App.

Finally we will discuss how you can take this new knowledge further.

Who developed Qlik Sense?

- Qlik Sense was developed by a Swedish company called QlikTech.

- QlikTech was founded in 1993.

- QlikTech has over 33,000 customers including Cisco, King, McAfee and many more.

- QlikTech has over 1600 Employees.

- Qlik Tech also developed a product call QlikView.

- The working title of Qlik Sense was Qlik.Next because it is seen as the next generation of QlikView.

If you have never heard of QlikView, QlikTech or Qlik Sense before then hopefully the points above should satisfy you that QlikTech is by no means a small company.

Next we will look at getting the software and installing it on your computer.

INSTALLATION OVERVIEW

What are the system requirements for Qlik Sense?

Below is a table of system requirements for Qlik Sense Desktop:

Operating System	Windows 7, 8.x (64-bit only)
Memory	4GB+
Disk space	500MB
Minimum Browser: Windows 7	IE 10, Chrome 24, Firefox 18
Minimum Browser: Windows 8 (not tablets)	IE 10, Chrome 24
Screen Resolution (minimum)	1024x768
.NET Framework	4.0

Where can I get the software and how much does it cost?

It's Free! , Go to:

http://www.qlik.com/us/explore/products/sense/desktop

Fill in the form and click on the 'Download Now' button to download the software.

The software will automatically download.

QLIK SENSE INSTALLATION

Next we will install the Qlik Sense Desktop.

The Qlik Sense Desktop is the application that will be used for the development and viewing of your qlik sense apps.

1. Double click on the downloaded file Qlik_Sense_ Desktop_setup.exe and click the run button:

2. Click on the install option, accept the license agreement and click next.

3. Click Install.

4. When the installation has completed click the Finish button.

5. Now click on the desktop icon to start Qlik Sense:

Qlik Sense
Desktop

SUMMARY

In this chapter we covered the system requirements for Qlik Sense and you have downloaded Qlik Sense Desktop and installed the application.

In the next chapter you will start using Qlik Sense and create your first application, importing the data into Qlik Sense and creating a chart from the data.

MY FIRST QLIK SENSE APP

OVERVIEW

In this chapter we are going to perform the following tasks:

- Import Excel data into a Qlik Sense App.

- Create a chart from the imported data.

- Display the data in a table.

- Create a table of calendar month names within the QlikView document so that there is a link between the imported data and this new table created within QlikView.

- Update the Chart and Table to display the month names.

IMPORT DATA INTO QLIK SENSE

1. Open the Qlik Sense Desktop by clicking the desktop shortcut or menu option.

2. You will be presented with a welcome message.

3. Click on the 'Create a new app' option.

4. Enter a name of 'My first app' and click create.

5. Click on the 'Open app' button and the application will be opened.

6. Drag and drop the 'random-data-excel.xls' file with the sample data onto the app.

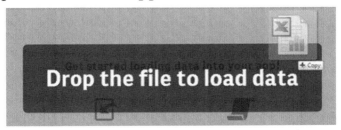

The following screen should appear:

7. Click on the 'Load data' button.

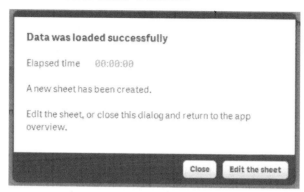

8. Click on the 'Edit the sheet' button to begin creating your first sheet.

Next we will create a simple bar chart and listbox based on the loaded data.

Sheet overview

The sheet in edit mode is split into various parts as shown:

Left pane - Assets pane

This has 3 main options shown in the last screenshot:

Charts option - which is selected - From here you can drag objects to the sheet.

Fields - Which shows all the available fields from the data model.

Master Items - These show Dimensions, Measures and Visualizations which have been setup to make the creation of objects such as chart easier.

Middle pane - sheet

The middle is the main design pane for creating and arranging your sheet objects.

Right pane - properties

The right side is the properties pane and defaults to the sheet properties.

If you require more space for the design pane click on the following icon in either the bottom left\right corner of the screen to hide the left\right pane.

Create the sheet objects

1. Drag and drop the 'Bar chart' icon to the middle part of the sheet.

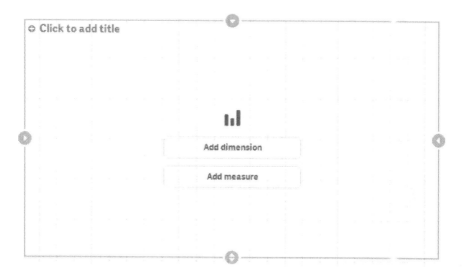

2. Click on the add dimension button and select the month field.

Dimensions

Dimensions determine how the data will be grouped in the chart (the X axis).

Measures

The measure will determine what value is plotted on the y-axis of the chart.

3. Click on the add measure button. Select the total field and then select the sum(TOTAL) aggregation.

4. Drag the 'Filter pane' option to the sheet.

5. Click the 'add dimension' option and select month.

6. Click 'Done' to view your first sheet.

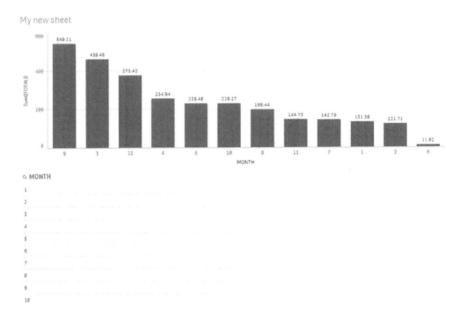

7. To display the label values on the bars expand the Appearance->Presentation section in the properties pane of the bar chart and set the 'Label Values' option to Auto.

8. Click the save button.

9. Now if you select a MONTH value from the MONTH filter pane the chart will be updated to only display the selected months.

Bar selection options

If you select one of the Months from the bar chart you will be presented with the following options.

The tick and cross are used to confirm or cancel the selection.

The dash line box with the cross is to clear the selection.

The first button on the left is to 'Turn on the lasso selection', this allows you to draw a shape around the bars you wish to select:

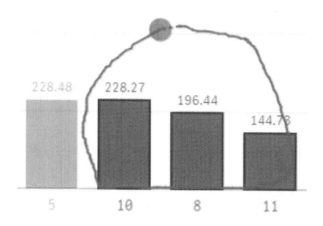

You can also select bars using the x and y axes by selecting and holding the mouse down on one of the axes and dragging the mouse to select some bars as shown:

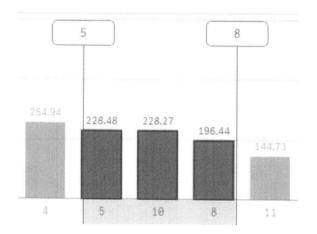

Filter selection options

Select an option on the month filter pane, then click the '...' button to display a menu with the following filtering options:

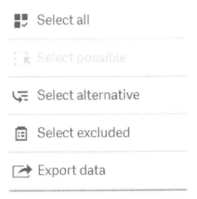

	Select all
	Select possible
	Select alternative
	Select excluded
	Export data

'Select possible' will select all the possible options ie: those that are still white.

'Select excluded' will select all the options that are dark gray.

'Select alternative', alternative values are those that where possible before the current selection was made.

For example if we select the month 9 (Sept) and Year 2010:

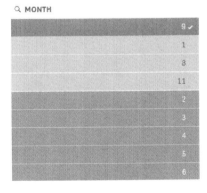

Here the alternative values are 1, 8 and 11.

Whereas other months have been excluded.

So choosing the option 'select alternative' will se.ect 1, 8 and 11 and unselect 9.

Completed App:

My first qlik sense app\My first app-completed.q\ f

DATA LOAD EDITOR (DLE)

In this book the Data Load Editor is often abbreviated to DLE.

Whereas the Data Model Viewer is abbreviated to DMV.

Just like when you editing a sheet the DLE is spl t into 3 main panes.

Left pane: Sections

The left pane is used to divide your loadscript into sections (In QlikView this was called tabs).

You just click on the + symbol at the top of the pane to add a new section.

Middle pane: The Loadscript

The Loadscript is the script you use to load data into your Qlik Sense app.

The middle pane contains the script for the currently selected section.

Each new document contains SET statements to create variables that contain standard values such as the MonthNames or DayNames for the system settings.

As you can probably tell from the MoneyFormat and DateFormat below the screenshot is a computer setup with the UK regional settings.

```
SET ThousandSep=',';
SET DecimalSep='.';
SET MoneyThousandSep=',';
SET MoneyDecimalSep='.';
SET MoneyFormat='£#,##0.00;-£#,##0.00';
SET TimeFormat='hh:mm:ss';
SET DateFormat='DD/MM/YYYY';
SET TimestampFormat='DD/MM/YYYY hh:mm:ss[.fff]';
SET MonthNames='Jan;Feb;Mar;Apr;May;Jun;Jul;Aug;Sep;Oct;Nov;Dec';
SET DayNames='Mon;Tue;Wed;Thu;Fri;Sat;Sun';
SET LongMonthNames='January;February;March;April;May;June;July;August;September;October;November;December';
SET LongDayNames='Monday;Tuesday;Wednesday;Thursday;Friday;Saturday;Sunday';
SET FirstWeekDay=0;
SET BrokenWeeks=1;
SET ReferenceDay=0;
SET FirstMonthOfYear=1;
```

Right pane: Create and Manage Connections

The right pane allows you create connections to data sources such as Access \ SQL databases using ODBC or OLEDB connections.

You also have the ability to select the data you wish to read into your app.

Bottom of screen

Output button

The output button at the bottom of the screen allows you to view the output of the last 'load data' command.

Top right

DEBUG AND LOAD DATA

The Load data button is used to run the current script and load data into your app.

The scripts are run from top to bottom in the order of the sections in the left pane.

The debug button is to the left of the load data button.

Click on the debug button to make Variables and Breakpoint buttons appear at the bottom of the screen next to the Output button.

VARIABLES

You can create a simple variable by adding the line of code:

LET mytestvar =1;

If you click on the 'load data' button the variable mytestvar will appear in the 'User defined variables' and 'All Variables' sections.

You can use the Variables dropdown menu to show certain variables: All, System, Reserved or User Defined.

You can click on the star next to the variable name to add it to your favourites variables which is useful if you have many variables in your app.

BREAKPOINTS

Breakpoints allow you to stop the loading of the script at a certain point, for example if you want to check the values of certain variables.

You can click to the right of a line of code in the same column as the row numbers to add a breakpoint as shown:

```
SET LongDayNames='Monday;Tuesday;
SET FirstWeekDay=0;
SET BrokenWeeks=1;
SET ReferenceDay=0;
SET FirstMonthOfYear=1;

LET mytestvar =1;
```

Breakpoint

```
LOAD * INLINE
    MONTH, MO
    1, Jan
    2, Feb
    3, Mar
    4, Apr
    5, May
```

Finally if you put a tick in the 'limited load' tickbox you can enter the number of lines you wish to read.

For example if we ticked the limited load and entered a value of 3 and click the play button we would see the following output.

Calendar << INL1E36

Lines fetched: 3

years_to_display

Lines fetched: 2

09:46:47

Sheet1$

Lines fetched: 3

This shows us that no more than 3 lines of each source where read.

NEW TAB OPTION - IN THE DLE

In the DLE you can open various commands in a new tab like you might in a web browser.

You do this by selecting the navigation button and then instead of clicking on the words 'App Overview' you click on the icon of 2 windows on the far right of the menu to open the option in a new tab.

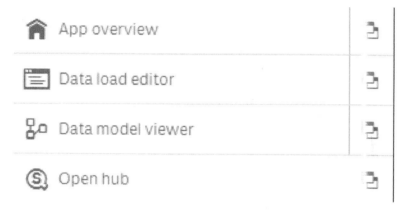

INLINE TABLES

A table that is defined and stored in the load script is called an Inline table.

Next we are going to add an Inline table so that we can convert the Month numbers into abbreviated month names such as Jan, Feb, Mar etc...

1. Select the Navigation button then the option 'Data load editor':

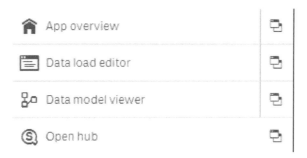

2. Type the following Inline table into the DLE script in the Main section (see data sources\calendar table.txt).

Calendar:

LOAD * INLINE [

Num, Name

1, Jan

2, Feb

3, Mar

4, Apr

5, May

6, Jun

7, Jul

8, Aug

9, Sep

10, Oct

11, Nov

12, Dec

];

3. You can add a name to this table by entering the table name followed by a colon in the line before the load statement. In this example we have called the table 'Calendar'.

IMPORTANT: Links between tables are created when field names are the same in both tables.

The main fields in the first table were:

ID

TOTAL

MONTH

YEAR

The inline table has the fields:

Num

Name

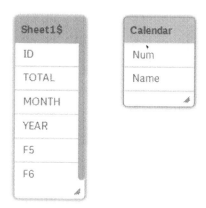

4. Qlik Sense would create no link between these tables, we can easily change the fieldnames on the inline table by just renaming the header names as in the example:

Calendar:

LOAD * INLINE [

MONTH, MONTHNAME

1, Jan

2, Feb

3, Mar

4, Apr

5, May

6, Jun

7, Jul

8, Aug

9, Sep

10, Oct

11, Nov

12, Dec

];

LOAD

ID,

"TOTAL",

"MONTH",

"YEAR",

F5,

F6

FROM 'lib://book source code/random-data-excel.xls'

(biff, embedded labels, table is Sheet1$);

5. We have changed the fields in this table from Num and Name to MONTH and MONTHNAME. Reload the data.

6. If we now go to the Data model viewer we can see that Qlik Sense has created a link between the 2 tables using the MONTH field.

Testing the Inline Table

Now update the dimension for the bar chart.

1. Open the sheet, 'My new sheet'.

2. Click the edit button.

3. Select the bar chart.

4. Click on the Data Section in the properties pane.

5. Expand the MONTH dimension and change the field name to MONTHNAME and press Enter.

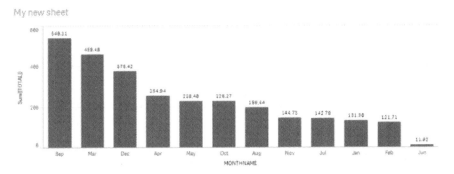

6. Select the MONTH Filter pane and change the dimension field to MONTHNAME, keeping the title as MONTH.

7. Save the sheet to prevent losing changes and view the results of your sheet.

Q **MONTH**

Jan

Feb

Mar

Apr

May

Completed App:

My first qlik sense app\My first app-monthname-completed.qvf

BASIC CONCEPTS

Next we will cover some of the concepts used in Ql k Sense and throughout this book.

Associative Experience

The Associative Experience is the core feature of Ql k Sense that allows the user to see which values are as ociated based on the data model using colors.

- Green is used for the values that have been selected by the user.

- White shows values that are associated with the current selection also called the possible values.

- Dark gray shows the values that are not associated with the current selection.

- Light gray values are alternative values. For example in a list this would be values that would be possible values if the selection within the field had not been made.

This experience of showing what values are related allows the user to quickly explore the data and answer questions they might have.

For example, in a Sales example you might want to find what products the top customers 5 customers used.

These types of questions would be easy to answer with Qlik Sense.

Desktop Hub

The desktop hub is where you will find all the apps that are available to you and from where you will create a new app.

On your computer the apps will be in the following folder:

C:\Users\<username>\Documents\Qlik\Sense\Apps

Sheet

A Qlik Sense App is made up of mainly Sheets, Bookmarks and Stories.

The sheet is where you will do the most of your qlik sense development and drag objects such as tables and charts to arranged and customized.

Master Items

Master items allow for global changes by creating reusable dimensions, measures and visualizations (such as charts).

Snapshots

Snapshots allow you to take screenshots of objects such as charts and tables to use later in your Stories.

You can highlight values in the snapshot when you add it to a slide.

Data Storytelling

This feature allows you to create slides that contain the snapshots, text and images.

You also can create a slide that contains a whole sheet with the ability to go back to the sheet from the slide.

Dimensions

Dimensions determine how the data will be grouped in the chart (the X axis).

Measures

The expression will determine what value is plotted on the y-axis of the chart.

Data Load Editor = DLE

In this book I have abbreviated the Data Load Editor to DLE.

The DLE is where you create the script to load the data into your qlik sense app and create the data model.

Getting the data model correct is the No1 important thing to get right with your Qlik Sense app.

You can create a simple UI and encourage users to create their own sheets but without a correct data model the app with be of little value to the user.

Data Model Viewer = DMV

The data model view allows you to view the data model that was created with the script in the DLE.

You can also preview the data that is contained within the tables to check it has been loaded into your app.

String or Field

When developing in qlik sense it is important to know that different types of quotes represent strings (sometimes called literals) or fieldnames:

Strings(literals) = ' '

Field name = "" or [] or ``

This is important when creating a field name in your script that contains spaces where you would use "" or [] or ``.

For example:

LOAD

'test' as "MY TEST FIELD"

AUTOGENERATE(1);

The data 'test' is contained within the field called "MY TEST

FIELD".

SUMMARY

Using a simple example we have covered:

- How to import data from an Excel spreadsheet.
- How to display data in a simple bar chart and a filter pane.
- How to create tables of data within your Qlik Sense document (Inline tables).
- How tables are linked together in Qlik Sense.
- In the next chapter we are going to look at the Qlik Sense app in more detail.
- We will look at some of the following areas:
- Different data sources that you can use.
- How you can change the imported data using expressions.
- Different types of Charts that you can use to display your data.
- Ways that you can filter the data in the load script using inner joins and the where clause.

PART 2

CREATING QLIK SENSE APPS

OVERVIEW

In this chapter we will describe:

- The types of files you can read data from into your Qlik Sense app.

- Demonstrate examples of importing data from Excel and Text files.

- How you can filter the data in your data model using inner joins.

READ DATA INTO QLIK SENSE
DATA SOURCES

A data source is where you are get the data you wish to analyze.

Different types of data sources need to be setup in different ways.

I will describe each of the main data sources for Qlik Sense.

The first data source you will have already encountered if you are following the examples is the Excel file.

Excel files are one of a group of files you can import into Qlik Sense called 'Table Files'.

1. From within the 'data load editor' click on the 'select data' button:

2. Then select the 'file type' dropdown list to see the table file options:

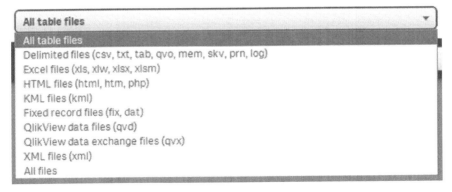

3. There are various other options for data sources you can see in the 'data load editor' by clicking on the 'create new connection' button.

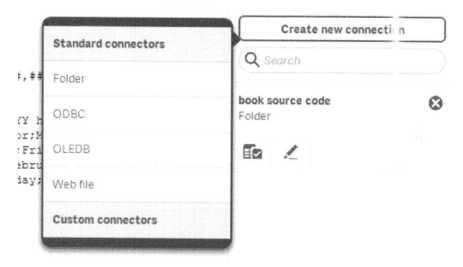

When starting to use Qlik Sense you will mostly use this option to import Excel or Delimited files such as csv (comma separated files) or plain text files such as a log.

TABLE FILES

EXCEL

This is the data source that everyone uses first when learning Qlik Sense.

There are various ways you can load Excel files into qlik sense.

DRAG AND DROP

Open the App and drag and drop the file onto the screen.

You can also drag and drop the spreadsheet onto a sheet.

If you already have data in the app you are asked if you would like to replace or add the data already loaded.

Each data file is created within a new tab in the data load editor.

SELECT DATA BUTTON

Within the data load editor click the 'select data' button and browse to the data file.

TABLE FILES - EXCEL EXAMPLE

1. Create a new app - called Customers.

2. Drag and drop the following file onto the app page:

SampleCustomerReports.xls

3. Under field names selected 'Embedded field names so the fieldnames within the data are used.

4. Click the 'load data' button.

5. When you get the message 'Data was loaded successfully', click close.

6. Click the save button then go to the 'data load editor' (DLE).

7. In the DLE a tab called 'SampleCustomerReports.xls.' is created with the following script:

LOAD

Product,

Customer,

"Qtr 1",

"Qtr 2",

"Qtr 3",

"Qtr 4"

FROM 'lib://data sources/SampleCustomerReports.xls'

(biff, embedded labels, table is [Source Data$]);

In your script the path to the spreadsheet might be different if it was stored in a different folder.

TEXT FILES

There are several reasons to import text files into Qlik Sense. For example all your data might be in a csv (comma separated value) format or you do not own Microsoft Office.

In this example we are going to import a list of years.

1. Create a simple text file with the following data called years_to_display.txt (see data sources folder in sample data):

   2009

   2010

2. Open the 'My first app' app created in Part1 or copy the app 'My first qlik sense app\My first app-inner join completed.qvf' to your Apps folder.

3. Edit the 'My new sheet' sheet.

4. Click on the fields in the left pane and drag the year field to the sheet as show (if it does not already exist):

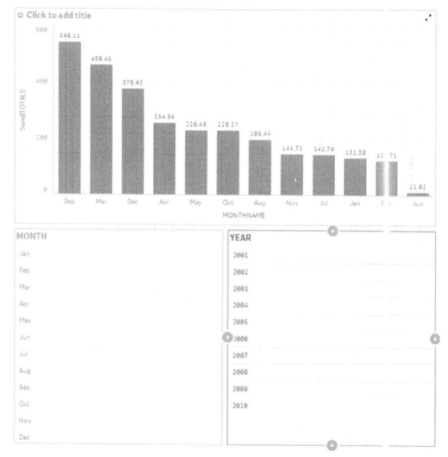

5. Drag and drop the file years_to_display.txt to the sheet:

6. Click Add data.

7. Click the header of the data and change @1 to YEAR and click 'Load data', then click 'Close':

Fields

☑ Select all fields

8. Go to the data load editor,

You should see the following code added to the years_to_display.txt tab:

LOAD

@1 as "YEAR"

FROM 'lib://source code/years_to_display.txt'

(txt, codepage is 1252, no labels, delimiter is '\t', msq);

INNER JOIN

If you wanted to display only the years listed in your text file you could create a join between the tables as in the following example:

To only display the years listed in the text file I added the following 'INNER JOIN' command before the SalesData table is read.3

INNER JOIN (years_to_display)

This command means that data will only be read from the SalesData table where there is a matching record in the years_to_display table.

In this case the years_to_display and SalesData tables are linked using the YEAR field so only years listed in the years_to_display table will be displayed.

The 'years to display' filter pane lists the records in the YEAR field.

1. Using the App created in the 'Text Files' example go to the DLE.

2. Click on the 3 bars to the left of the section name

'random-data-excel.xls' and when you see the crosshairs click the left mouse and drag the tab to move the random-data-excel.xls tab to the bottom as shown:

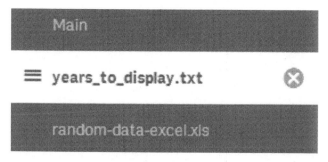

3. Add the inner join as shown and click 'Load data':

INNER JOIN (years_to_display)

LOAD

ID,

"TOTAL",

"MONTH",

"YEAR",

F5,

F6

FROM 'lib://book source code/random-data-excel.xls'

(biff, embedded labels, table is Sheet1$);

4. Go back to the 'my first sheet' to see the filtered data:

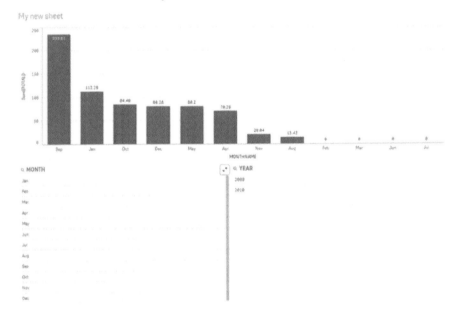

Completed App:

My first qlik sense app\My first app-inner join completed. qvf

PART 3

MANAGE DATA

OVERVIEW

In this chapter of the book we will focus on the data that is being brought into your Qlik Sense app.

We will cover:

- Reading data from ODBC and OLE DB connections.

- Managing the data such as creating links between 2 tables or reading less data using the WHERE clause.

- Creating expressions to calculate fields and also some useful expressions to know when loading data into your app.

- Some useful functions such as concat and count functions.

- Using Folder connections.

MANAGE DATA LOADED INTO QLIK SENSE

Once you have created the right links between your tables creating the charts\tables from that data is relatively easy.

In this chapter we will examine how Qlik Sense creates links between tables and how we can prevent Qlik Sense from creating unwanted links between tables.

We will also cover the use of expressions in Qlik Sense to manage your data.

Next we will look at how you can preview the data you have loaded into your Qlik Sense app using your load script.

You can explore the data you have loaded by going to the Navigation Menu then selecting the 'Data model viewer' (DMV) option.

This is the table that we used in the previous example of an ODBC connection to an Access database.

For a more complex view of several tables linked together see the next screenshot.

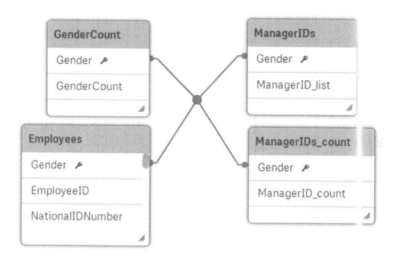

CIRCULAR REFERENCES

When you load data that contains a circular reference you will get the following warning:

(I'm sure references to QlikView will be replaced with Qlik Sense eventually)

Finished with error(s) and/or warning(s)

Circular reference: One or more loops have been detected in your database structure. Loops may cause ambiguous results and should therefore be avoided. QlikView will cut the loop(s) automatically by setting one or more tables as loosely coupled. Use Loosen Table script statement to explicitly declare loosely coupled tables.

Go to the DMV and you will see the data model that has been loaded:

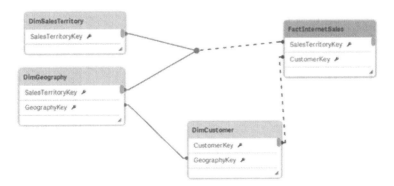

NOTE: The tables with links between the fields have the same field name.

Dashed lines in the DMV means that there is a Circular reference between tables.

The problem with circular references is that they can lead to unpredictable results.

The example below shows the links between tables that cause a circular reference:

DimCustomer(GeographyKey) ->
DimGeography(GeographyKey)

DimGeography(SalesTerritory) ->
FactInternetSales(SalesTerritory)

Back to:

FactInternetSales(CustomerKey) ->
DimCustomer(CustomerKey)

To avoid Circular references firstly you need to decide if we need all the fields in each table.

If you can remove fields from the load script that are not required this might break the circular reference.

If all fields are required we can make changes to the way tables are linked together using the QUALIFY statement which we will cover next.

LINK TABLES

Qlik Sense creates links between tables of data where there are identical field names in both tables. It is that simple.

But with that simplicity there can sometimes be problems that need to be resolved.

Such as when Qlik Sense creates a link between 2 tables that you do not want.

Luckily there are a couple of ways that we can fix these problems:

Using the AS clause to rename field names. The format of the AS clause is:

<original fieldname> AS <new fieldname>

1. Click on the 'Qlik Sense Desktop hub' tab and click 'Create new app'.

2. Create a new app called 'link example'.

3. Click open app.

4. Drag and drop the users.txt file into the app.

5. For the 'Field names' dropdownlist select 'Embedded field names'.

6. Click 'load data'.

7. Click close, then click Save (Ctrl+S).

8. Go to Navigation -> Data Model viewer to check the users table was loaded.

9. Click on the Preview bar at the bottom of the screen to check the data:

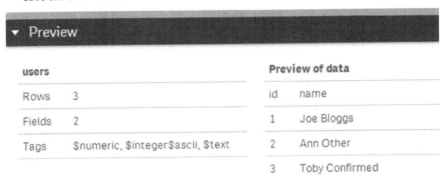

10. Next drag and drop the customers.txt file onto the Data Model viewer page.

11. Select 'Add data' and as before for the 'Field names' dropdownlist select 'Embedded field names' and click 'Load data'.

12. Click 'load data'.

13. Click close, then click Save (Ctrl+S).

14. Go to Navigation - Data Model viewer to check the customers table was loaded. A single table (users) exists because same field names as users table and both tables are automatically concatenated together.

15. Next go to the 'data load editor' and add table names the load statements:

Your scripts in the users.txt and customers tab should be the same as below:

appUsers:

LOAD

id,

name

FROM 'lib://manage data/users.txt'

(txt, codepage is 1252, embedded labels, delimiter is ',', msq);

appCustomers:

LOAD

id,

name

FROM 'lib://manage data/customers.txt'

(txt, codepage is 1252, embedded labels, delimiter is ',', msq);

16. Click load data, then close. Go to the data model viewer and see the 2 files have been loaded into 1 table called users.

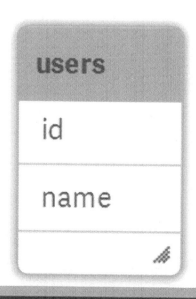

Preview of data

id	name
1	Joe Bloggs
2	Ann Other
3	Toby Confirmed
1	United Limited
2	Global inc
3	PracticalQlik Plc

17. Go to the data load editor and add a NoConcatenate keyword before the LOAD statement.

appCustomers:

NoConcatenate LOAD

id,

name

FROM 'lib://manage data/customers.txt'

(txt, codepage is 1252, embedded labels, delimiter is ',', msq);

18. Click load data, notice 1 synthetic key has been created.

Data load progress

Data load is complete.

Elapsed time   00:00:00

```
Started loading data

appUsers << users
Lines fetched: 3
appCustomers << customers
Lines fetched: 3
$Syn 1 = id+name


App saved

Finished with error(s) and/or warning(s)

0 forced error(s)

1 synthetic key(s)
```

19. Click close and go to the Data Model Viewer.

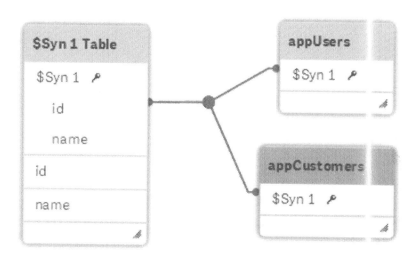

SEE APP:

Manage data\Manage data loaded into Qlik Ser se\link example1.qvf

20. For example: If you had the 2 tables below in your load script.

The 2 tables would be linked together because of the identical field names.

Therefore you can simply change name of the fields that are causing the link in one table as we have done in the appUsers table.

appUsers:

LOAD

id as userid,

name as username

FROM 'lib://manage data/users.txt'

(txt, codepage is 1252, embedded labels, delimiter is ',', msq);

appCustomers:

NoConcatenate LOAD

id,

name

FROM 'lib://manage data/customers.txt'

(txt, codepage is 1252, embedded labels, delimiter is ',', msq);

21. Now when you go to the DMV you will see there are no links between the 2 tables.

SEE APP:

Manage data\Manage data loaded into Qlik Sense\link example2.qvf

USE THE QUALIFY STATEMENT

This works by prefixing the table name to each field:

1. Add the following line to the end of the main tab

QUALIFY *;

2. Click Load data and close

3. Go to the DMV to see the fields now have a preview of the table name.

If you need to link the tables you can use the UNQUALIFY statement to prevent the table name from being prefixed to the field listed in the UNQUALIFY statement.

As in the next example where the id field is linked by using the UNQUALIFY statement.

1. Add the following to the end of the main tab:

UNQUALIFY id;

2. Click Load data and close

3. Go to the DMV to see the fields now have a preview of the table name except the id field.

SEE APP: Manage data\Manage data loaded into Qlik Sense\link example3.qvf

ODBC CONNECTION TO AN ACCESS DATABASE

In many respects this example is similar to the ODBC connection to the SQL server database.

But not everyone uses SQL server.

Get the Sample Data

1. Download and unzip the file AdventureWorks.zip from www.techstuffy.com/downloads.

The AdventureWorks.zip contains the access database AdventureWorks.accdb.

2. Open the ODBC Administrator. You will find this option in the Control Panel.

3. Sample scripts will be in:

Manage data\ODBC Connection to an Access database

ODBC Administrator

4. Click Start, then Control Panel\System and Security\ Administrative Tools then Data Sources (ODBC).

If you have the choice between 32-bit\64-bit ODBC Administrator you can choose either but will need to make the same selection when creating the new connection in the DLE.

Add a DSN for Microsoft Access

5. Click on the 'System DSN' tab. Click the Add button.

6. Highlight the 'Microsoft Access Driver (*.mdb, *.accdb)' option, then click 'Finish'.

7. The 'ODBC Microsoft Access Setup' screen will be displayed.

8. Click the 'Select' button and browse to your Access database.

9. Click the OK button.

10. Give your DSN a name such as: my_test_access_db.

11. Click the OK button.

You now can see your new DSN for Microsoft Access in the list of System DSNs.

Use the ODBC DSN

12. Now open Qlik Sense, click 'create a new app' and enter a name of 'AdventureWorks'.

13. Click create then Open App.

14. Open the data load editor.

15. Click on the 'Create new connection' option in the right pane and select ODBC.

16. Select the dsn my_test_access_db

17. Enter a name of my_test_access_db and click save.

18. A connection has been created as shown:

19 Click the first icon on the left under the connection to insert the connection string. In this example the following line is added to the cursor position:

LIB CONNECT TO 'my_test_access_db';

20. You can click 'Load data' to check that the connection string works.

Select Tables from your Access database

1. Click on the middle icon to 'Select Data' to display the following screen:

2. Select the table HumanResources_Employee.

3. You can filter the tables using the search box, in the screenshot I have entered the work Human.

4. Then hover over the tablenames and select the HumanResources_Employee table (see humanresources_employee.txt).

5. Click Insert Script to add the following script:

LIB CONNECT TO 'my_test_access_db';

LOAD EmployeeID,

NationalIDNumber,

ContactID,

LoginID,

ManagerID,

Title,

BirthDate,

MaritalStatus,

Gender,

HireDate,

SalariedFlag,

VacationHours,

SickLeaveHours,

CurrentFlag,

rowguid,

ModifiedDate;

SQL SELECT EmployeeID,

NationalIDNumber,

ContactID,

LoginID,

ManagerID,

Title,

BirthDate,

MaritalStatus,

Gender,

HireDate,

SalariedFlag,

VacationHours,

SickLeaveHours,

CurrentFlag,

rowguid,

ModifiedDate

FROM `HumanResources_Employee`;

7. Click Load data, once the data has loaded click close.

8. Click Navigation -> Data Model Viewer to view the data model.

9. Click Navigation -> App Overview and select 'Create new sheet'

10. Enter a sheet title of HumanResources.

11. Click on the new sheet and select Edit.

12. Click on the Fields option in the assets (left) pane, drag the following fields to the sheet:

EmployeeID

ContactID

Gender

13. Click Done.

14. Select EmployeeID 1.

15. Click on the green tick to confirm the selection.

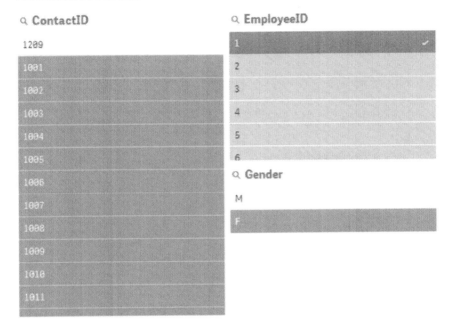

The fields that are not greyed out in the other list boxes tell me that this Employee has a Contract ID of 1209 and Gender is Male ('M').

Next we will look at how to manage the data you have loaded into your document.

16. Click on the save button.

Completed App:

Manage data\ODBC Connection to an Access database\

AdventureWorks-initial.qvf

ADD SOME EXPRESSIONS

Why add expressions to your apps?

You have already used simple expressions such as SUM(TOTAL) to calculate the total of some field.

The more complex your apps become the more you will find yourself asking questions that cannot be solved without using expressions.

We will start by using simple expressions to create calculated fields in the load script.

For example if you wanted to set a field to a different value if it was over some threshold.

Where can I use expressions?

Expressions can be used in various places within your Qlik Sense app.

The examples we are going to cover here are using expressions within:

- Loadscript – You can use expressions to calculate the value of fields.

- Measures – Each expression is calculated for each dimension.

- Other Objects – Most objects use expressions in some way.

For example you can add a measure to a 'Text & Image' object with the following expression:

='Gender count = ' &sum(GenderCount)

Which will display the following text when nothing is selected:

Gender count = 9

Be aware that the field names are case sensitive so that Gendercount is not the same as GenderCount.

If you make an error such as forgetting a bracket an error message will be displayed in the bottom left corner of the expression editor:

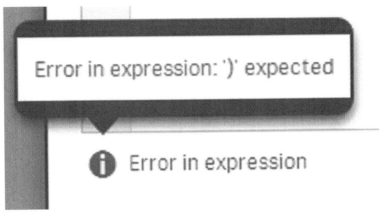

Expressions in the Load Script

In this example I will show how to create a calculated field in the load script.

1. Go to the DLE.

2. In the example below we are using the IF statement to calculate convert the Gender field so that M is converted to Male and F to Female.

3. The Format of the IF statement is:

IF(<EXPRESSION>, <TRUE VALUE>,<FALSE VALUE>) as <FIELDNAME>

4. The expression must be either true or false, in this example the expression is:

Gender='M'

5. The TRUE and FALSE values are strings within single quotes. The full IF statement is:

IF(Gender='M','Male','Female') as Gender

6. So if the Gender field is M, the field is set to 'Male', if not it will be set to 'Female'.

7. Here is an example of the statement from the load script.

To save on space we have replaced the list of fields with a * (this is not best practise as the fields read might change dramatically and you only want to read the data you need),

We have added the fields to the LOAD statement so we can change the Gender field using an IF statement.

Employees:

LOAD

EmployeeID,

NationalIDNumber,

ContactID,

LoginID,

ManagerID,

Title,

BirthDate,

MaritalStatus,

IF(Gender='M','Male','Female') as Gender,

HireDate,

SalariedFlag,

VacationHours,

SickLeaveHours,

CurrentFlag,

rowguid,

ModifiedDate;

SQL SELECT *

FROM `HumanResources_Employee`

WHERE EmployeeID<10;

8. Click the load data and go to the DMV to preview the data.

9. You should see the field has now been updated to either Male or Female.

Preview of data

Gender	EmployeeID	NationalIDNumber	ContactID	LoginID	ManagerID
Male	1	14417807	1209	adventure-works\guy1	16
Male	2	253022876	1030	adventure-works\kevin0	6
Male	3	509647174	1002	adventure-works\roberto0	12
Male	4	112457891	1290	adventure-works\rob0	3
Male	5	480168528	1009	adventure-works\thierry0	263
Male	6	24756624	1028	adventure-works\david0	109
Female	7	309738752	1070	adventure-works\jolynn0	21

10. You can also place calculated fields within the SQL SELECT statement, for example:

LOAD

ProductKey,

OrderDateKey,

UnitPrice,

OrderQuantity,

CustomerPONumber;

SQL SELECT *,

UnitPrice * OrderQuantity as TotalPrice

FROM AdventureWorksDW.dbo.FactInternetSales;

READ LESS DATA

You might not require all the data in the spreadsheet\text file\database that you are loading into your Qlik Sense app.

Next we will cover ways in which you can filter and group your data. If you have used SQL commands before these concepts will be familiar to you.

Filter the data: WHERE

The WHERE clause can be used with SQL SELECT statements.

1. Open up the AdventureWorks app you have already created.

2. Go to the DLE

In this example we are only reading the EmployeeIDs that are less than 10.

3. Add the following where clause to the end of your load statement for the HumanResources_Employee table and move the semi-colon to the end of the statement:

WHERE EmployeeID<10;

Your load statement should look like the following script:

(see read less data.txt in the data source sample data folder)

LIB CONNECT TO 'my_test_access_db';

LOAD EmployeeID,

NationalIDNumber,

ContactID,

LoginID,

ManagerID,

Title,

BirthDate,

MaritalStatus,

Gender,

HireDate,

SalariedFlag,

VacationHours,

SickLeaveHours,

CurrentFlag,

rowguid,

ModifiedDate;

SQL SELECT EmployeeID,

NationalIDNumber,

ContactID,

LoginID,

ManagerID,

Title,

BirthDate,

MaritalStatus,

Gender,

HireDate,

SalariedFlag,

VacationHours,

SickLeaveHours,

CurrentFlag,

rowguid, ModifiedDate

FROM `HumanResources_Employee`

WHERE EmployeeID<10;

NOTE: When adding a WHERE clause to your SQL SELECT statement remember to move the ';' to the end of the WHERE clause.

4. Click on the load data button and check that the 'lines fetched' is 9.

5. If the output of the load closes you can still click on the output button at the bottom left corner of the screen to see the result of the load. For example:

App successfully saved.

Started loading data

Connecting to my_test_access_db

Connected

HumanResources_Employee

Lines fetched: 9

App saved

Finished successfully

0 forced error(s)

0 synthetic key(s)

Grouping data: GROUP BY

In this example we will show how you can group data for example we can group the number of Employees by Gender using the code below.

1. Place this code below the script for the Employee table.

GenderCount:

LOAD

Gender,

COUNT(Gender) as GenderCount

Resident Employees

GROUP BY Gender;

The RESIDENT command specifies that you are using a table that has already been loaded into memory.

2. Add a table name of Employees to the LOAD statement as shown below:

LIB CONNECT TO 'my_test_access_db';

Employees:

LOAD *;

SQL SELECT EmployeeID,

NationalIDNumber,

ContactID,

LoginID,

ManagerID,

Title,

BirthDate,

MaritalStatus,

Gender,

HireDate,

SalariedFlag,

VacationHours,

SickLeaveHours,

CurrentFlag,

rowguid,

ModifiedDate

FROM `HumanResources_Employee`

WHERE EmployeeID<10;

GenderCount:

LOAD

Gender,

COUNT(Gender) as GenderCount

Resident Employees

GROUP BY Gender;

3. Click the load data button.

The output should show that the GenderCount table has 2 rows:

Employees << HumanResources_Employee

Lines fetched: 9

GenderCount << Employees

Lines fetched: 2

App saved

4. Go to the DMV.

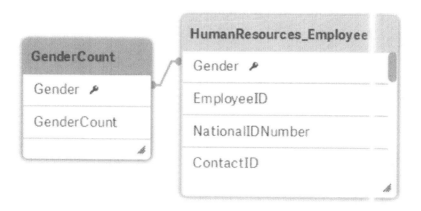

5. Preview the data as shown to see that we now have a count of the employees grouped by gender.

Preview of data

Gender	GenderCount
M	6
F	3

Completed App:

Manage data\Manage data loaded into Qlik Sense\

AdventureWorks-after gender count.qvf

USEFUL SCRIPT FUNCTIONS

Here we will cover some of the more useful scripting functions that are available in Qlik Sense.

Sum

This function calculates the total value.

Ie: Sum(OrderTotal) – might calculate the sum of all orders.

If the expression Sum(OrderTotal) was used in a chart as a measure with a Dimension of Customer you would calculate the total amount of orders for each customer.

Min\Max

These functions calculate the smallest and largest values in a set of numbers.

For example to find the min number for SickLeaveHours.

Load Gender, min(SickLeaveHours) as Min_ SickLeaveHours

From MyTable

group by Gender;

FirstValue\ LastValue

These functions calculate the first and last strings in load order. An example of this function is:

FirstValue(EmployeeID) as first_employee_loaded

Concat

This function can concatenate fields together. The concat function must be used with the GROUP BY clause.

This example concatenates the MangerID field separated by a ';'.

CONCAT(ManagerID,';') as ManagerID_list

Concat example

1. Open the AdventureWorks app, and go to the DLE.

2. Create a new tab called Managers and add the following code:

ManagerIDs:

LOAD

Gender,

CONCAT(ManagerID,';') as ManagerID_list

Resident Employees

GROUP BY Gender;

3. Below is a full example:

LIB CONNECT TO 'my_test_access_db';

Employees:

LOAD

EmployeeID,

NationalIDNumber,

ContactID,

LoginID,

ManagerID,

Title,

BirthDate,

MaritalStatus,

IF(Gender='M','Male','Female') as Gender,

HireDate,

SalariedFlag,

VacationHours,

SickLeaveHours,

CurrentFlag,

rowguid,

ModifiedDate;

SQL SELECT *

FROM `HumanResources_Employee`

WHERE EmployeeID<10;

ManagerIDs:

LOAD

Gender,

CONCAT(ManagerID,';') as ManagerID_list

Resident Employees

GROUP BY Gender;

4. In this example the concat field is grouped by Gender to display a list of manager's ids for each Gender.

A preview of the results in the DMV.

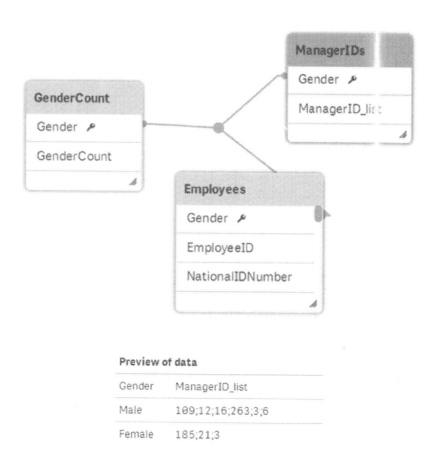

Count Functions

Count

The COUNT function – calculates the number of records by the GROUP BY clause.

1. The example shown here counts the number of ManagerID records by Gender:

ManagerIDs_count:

LOAD

Gender,

COUNT(ManagerID) as ManagerID_count

Resident Employees

GROUP BY Gender;

2. To test this add the code to the end of the Managers tab and click the load data button.

Preview of data

Gender	ManagerID_count
Male	6
Female	3

Completed App:

Manage data\Manage data loaded into Qlik Sense\ AdventureWorks-after gender count.qvf

3. If you add the distinct keyword only unique records will be counted, for example:

COUNT(DISTINCT ManagerID)

Date Functions

day() - Returns the day when passed a date

month() - Returns the month when passed a date

year() - Returns the year when passed a date.

GMT( ) - returns the current date\time for Greenwich Mean Time.

As you will see in later examples these functions are very useful for grouping data when using aggregation functions as well as exploring data.

Alt – Provide an alternative

This function provides the first valid number in the list.

If no valid number is found the last parameter is returned.

For example:

Alt ('add','ddd',23,'Error with variables')

This function is especially useful when using variables to check date formats.

FOLDER CONNECTIONS

When creating a loadscript to read data from files it is useful to create a folder connection to reuse again as a path to your files.

If you drag and drop your file such as an Excel spreadsheet onto your app the folder connection will be created automatically with a connection name of the folder that contains the file.

So if you drag and drop a spreadsheet from the 'data sources' folder that contains the spreadsheet sample data for this book the folder connection name will also be 'data sources'.

1. Create a new app called 'folderconn' and Go to the DLE.

2. Select 'Create new connection' and select Folder

3. Enter a name for the folder: data sources.

4. Click save. A connection will be created.

data sources
Folder

5. Now you can click the 'select data' button and choose a file within the folder that you wish to read into the app.

6. Click Select once you have chosen the file.

7. Then click Insert script and the script will be added to the position of the cursor in the loadscript, for example:

LOAD

Product,

Customer,

"Qtr 1",

"Qtr 2",

"Qtr 3",

"Qtr 4"

FROM 'lib://data sources/SampleCustomerReports.xls'

(biff, embedded labels, table is [Source Data$]);

8. Notice that the path to the spreadsheet uses the location of the data sources data connection, this is similar to using variables to store the paths to your data source files.

9. If you are using the sample apps that are available with this book you will probably have to edit the folder connection for the 'data sources' or 'qvd data' connections so that they are in the location where you have saved your sample data.

PART 4

CHARTS AND TABLES

OVERVIEW

As someone who does not like typing once said "a picture is worth a thousand words" (or it might have been a photo journalist).

So in this section of the book there will be plenty of pictures or as we will be calling them 'Charts'.

In this section I will concentrate of the most popular types of charts that you will be creating in your Qlik Sense application.

WHAT TYPES OF CHARTS CAN I CREATE?

Most tools for analyzing data have a variety of Charts that can be created and Qlik Sense is no exception. In this part of the book we will be covering:

- Bar chart
- Line chart
- Pie chart
- Tables
- Chart Expression and Groups

Other charts that we will cover in the Advanced Topics part later in this book:

- Combo chart
- Gauge
- Scatter plot
- Tree map

In the chapter 'My First Qlik Sense App' we demonstrated how to create a Bar chart. Next we start by looking at the Table object.

TABLES

1. From the Desktop hub, create a new app called Charts and open the app.

2. Drag and drop the following spreadsheet to the app to load the data: SampleCustomerReports.xls.

3. Select 'Embedded field names' for the field names option.

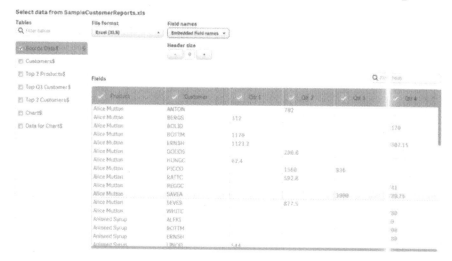

4. Click Load data.

5. Click Edit the sheet and click the save button.

6. Next we are going to add some dimensions and measures to the master items to make the tables\charts easier to create.

7. Click on the master items option and click Dimensions:

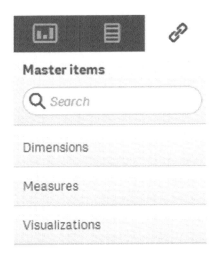

8. Click create new and then select the Customer field.

9. Add a description and tag for the customer dimension as shown:

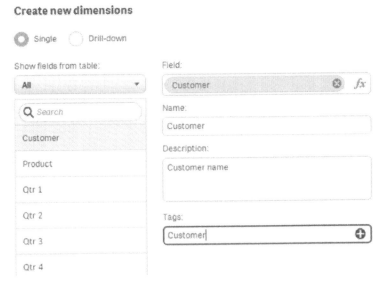

10. You can add tags to items such as dimension and

measures to make them easier to search. Click 'Add dimension'.

11. Click the product field and click 'add dimension, then click done.

12. Click the Measures option, then 'Create new'.

13. Click on the Fx to open the expression editor.

14. Select the field Qtr 1 and aggregation of Sum, then click Insert.

This will create the following expression:

Sum([Qtr 1])

15. Click Apply

16. Add a name, description and tag for the measure as shown:

17. Use a tag of qtr_sum for each measure.

18. Create the same Sum measures for Qtr2, Qtr3 and Qtr4 fields.

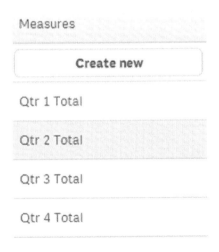

19. In the master items search box try searching for qtr_ sum which should display all measures with the qtr_ sum tag.

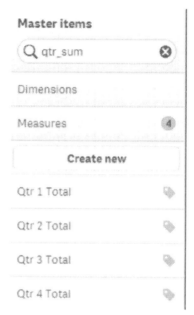

CREATE THE TABLE

1. Click on the charts icon.

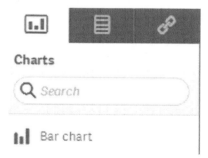

2. Drag and drop the Table chart to the sheet.

3. Click 'Add Dimension' on the table and select Customer.

4. Select the table.

5. Click on the Data section in the properties (right) pane and click 'Add column'.

6. Select measure and choose the 'Qtr 1 Total' measure.

7. Click the add column again and repeat this to add the following measures:

'Qtr 2 Total'

'Qtr 3 Total'

'Qtr 4 Total'

8. Resize the table using the arrows in orange circles so that you can see all the columns.

9. Click the Save button.

10. Click on the table title and add the title 'Quarterly Sales Figures'

11. Click on the Sheet name and rename the Title to 'Sales' in the properties pane.

12. Click 'Done', then click Save to view your work so far which should look like the following screenshot:

Sales

Quarterly Sales Figures

Customer	Qtr 1 Total	Qtr 2 Total	Qtr 3 Total	Qtr 4 Total
Totals	138288.9	143177.02	153937.73	181681.43
ALFKI	0	0	814.5	1208
ANATR	0	0	479.75	320
ANTON	0	4771.91	1188.86	0
AROUT	407.7	2142.9	0	3856.3
BERGS	1206.6	4693.73	5920.68	2028
BLAUS	0	615.8	464	0
BLONP	3832.72	2875.16	1110	0
BOLID	0	0	0	3026.85

13. Notice the magnifier glass next to the customer column and click on it to filter the rows in the table by customer.

14. Click with the left mouse to make multiple selections, no need to hold the shift\ctrl keys to make multiple selections.

15. Edit the sheet and select the table.

16. Click add column in the properties pane and select dimension and Product. Collapse all the column details as shown:

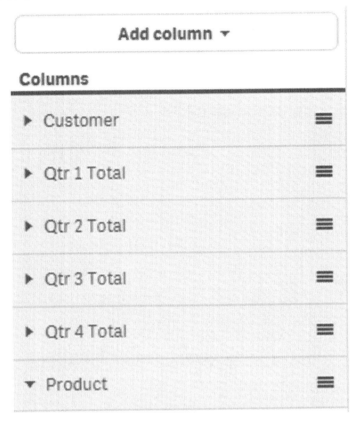

17. Now you can click on the column title, hold the left mouse and drag the column to reorder the columns.

18. Move the Product column to be after the customer column as in the previous screenshot. Click Save and then Done to view the results:

Sales

Quarterly Sales Figures

Customer	Product	Qtr 1 Total	Qtr 2 Total	Qtr 3 Total	Qtr 4 Total
Totals		£138,288.90	£143,177.02	£153,937.73	£1,681.43
ALFKI	Aniseed Syrup	£0.00	£0.00	£0.00	£60.00
ALFKI	Lakkalikööri	£0.00	£0.00	£0.00	£270.00
ALFKI	Vegie-spread	£0.00	£0.00	£0.00	£878.00
ALFKI	Spegesild	£0.00	£0.00	£18.00	£0.00
ALFKI	Chartreuse verte	£0.00	£0.00	£283.50	£0.00
ALFKI	Rössle Sauerkraut	£0.00	£0.00	£513.00	£0.00
ANATR	Mascarpone Fabioli	£0.00	£0.00	£0.00	£320.00
ANATR	Tofu	£0.00	£0.00	£69.75	£0.00

MORE TABLE DETAILS

Next we will look at more ways to customize the 'Quarterly Sales Figures' table.

1. Go to the Sales sheet and click the edit button and select the 'Quarterly Sales Figures' table.

2. Expand the screen so you can see all the columns in the table.

There are 3 sections in the right pane.

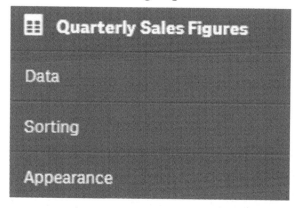

Columns

Dimension Columns

1. Click on the 'Data' column section to expand it.

2. Then click on the Customer column.

You have the option to display or hide NULL values, ie: where no value exists.

You can also use the Limitation dropdown list, to limit the dimensions displayed.

Fixed Number

You can display the top\bottom number of values, for example if we selected top 3 we would get the top 3 customers in the table.

Exact Number

The 'Exact Number' option allows you to limit the number of values using operators such as:

>= greater or equal to

> greater than

< less than

<= less than or equal to.

You could add an expression for example: =sum([Qtr 1])>0

Which would display all the rows where the 'Qtr 1 Total' was greater than zero.

Relative Value

Display the relative amount in percent using the same operators as for the Exact number.

Show Others

This value groups all the values not displayed. The default label is 'Others'.

Set the Customer column back to 'no limitation'.

Measures Columns

1. Click on the 'Qtr 1 Total' column.

We have already set the number formatting for these columns to 'Money'.

Notice the format pattern (this is region specific so if you are in the US for example you will get dollar signs).

An example of the format is displayed below the pattern:

£#,##0.00;-£#,##0.00

You could change the pattern here to take affect, it just defaults to the regional settings.

2. For example I could change the pattern to use the dollar simply by changing the pattern to:

$#,##0.00;-£#,##0.00

Qtr 1 Total	Qtr 2 Total
$138,288.90	£143,177.02
$0.00	£0.00
$0.00	£0.00
$0.00	£0.00
$0.00	£0.00
$0.00	£0.00
$0.00	£0.00

If we look at the pattern, ignoring the currency symbol:

£#,##0.00;-£#,##0.00

The pattern is split into 2 by a semi-colon, 1 pattern for positive and another for negative values.

Looking at the positive pattern:

#,##0.00

0 = one value.

= one possible value.

At the very least this pattern will show 1 value before the decimal point and 2 after.

There will be a comma as a thousand separator.

Background color expression

You can use colours such as red(),blue() or green().

You can also use the rgb() combined with an if statement to set the background colour in the table conditionally:

1. In the background color expression field for 'Qtr 1 Total', enter the following expression:

if([Qtr 1]>0,rgb(0,255,0))

Qtr 1 Total
£138,288.90
£137.70
£0.00
£0.00
£312.00
£0.00
£0.00
£0.00

2. Click done and scroll down the table or click on the 'Qtr 1 Total' column header to sort the table.

SORTING

1. Click on the Sorting section.

You can drag the columns into the order you wish them to be sorted by left clicking the column and dragging it to the desired position.

In this example I have moved the Product column to be the second column after the Customer.

2. If you click on one of the columns within the Sorting section you will see more options:

Change the Sorting field from Auto to Custom by clicking on the slider:

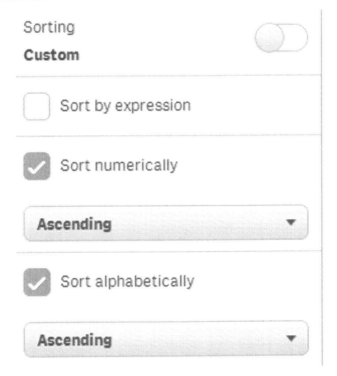

Here you can select:

Sort by expression

Sort numerically - either Ascending \ Descending

Sort alphabetically - either Ascending \ Descending

3. Expand the Sorting option for the Product column.

Take the tick out of Sort numerically and alphabetically.

4. Tick the Sort by expression option and enter the following expression to calculate the sum of all the quarters:

=Sum([Qtr 1])+Sum([Qtr 2])+Sum([Qtr 3])+Sum([Qtr 4])

5. Click Done.

6. Select the Customer ALFKI

7. You should see that the Products for the customer have been sorted by the total sales from the 4 quarters.

8. Click Save.

9. Click Edit.

APPEARANCE

In the appearance section, you can make the following changes to your table:

- You can turn the titles on\off.

- Change the title.

- In edit mode the title can also be changed by click on the title on the table.

- Add a subtitle.

- Change location of the Totals and the label for the Totals row.

For example:

Sales

Quarterly Sales Figures

Data from Excel (subtitle)

Customer Q	Product
Totals	
ALFKI	Rössle Sauerkraut
ALFKI	Lakkalikööri
ALFKI	Vegie-spread
ALFKI	Chartreuse verte
ALFKI	Spegesild
ALFKI	Aniseed Syrup
ANATR	Camembert Pierrot

For Demo purposes only (footnote)

You can also select the position of the totals to be the top\ bottom or auto selected.

Completed app:

Charts and Tables\Tables\Charts-tables-completed.qvf

BAR CHART

Now we will move onto the more common chart types, first the bar chart. Although we have created Bar charts already we will now focus on some of the other options available.

Starting app:

Charts and Tables\Tables\Charts-tables-completed.qvf

1. Open the Charts app and edit the Sales sheet.

2. Drag a bar chart object to the bottom of the sheet.

3. Click 'add dimension' and select Customer.

4. Click add measure and select Qtr 1 Total.

5. Add a title of 'Q1 Sales Totals', by clicking on the chart title and typing the title.

Notice that under the chart you have a slider that allows you to slide across the x axes by dragging the box left or right.

6. Edit the sheet again and select the chart.

Now we will focus on the right pane and some the details that are particular to charts.

Some of the parameters that the bar chart has in common with the table object:

- Dimensions.
- Limitations.
- Measures - Number formatting.
- Sorting - ordering the data numerically, alphabetically or by some expression.
- Appearance -> General

Just like the Table you can set the:

- Title
- Subtitle
- Footnote

ADD-ONS

Data handling

Show zero values - hide\show zero values in the bar chart.

7. Untick this box to remove zero value bars.

Reference lines

8. Click Add reference line.

9. Add a label of 'Average'.

10. Add and expression of:

=avg([Qtr 1])

11. In the properties pane set the presentation -> values labels -> to Auto.

12. Click Done and click Save.

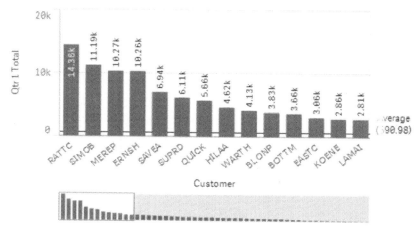

Completed app:

Charts and Tables\ Bar Chart\ Charts-after ref line.qvf

Appearance

Presentation

In the Presentation section you can:

- Set the orientation to either Vertical\ Horizontal

(default:Vertical).

- Grid line spacing (default:auto).

- You can set the grid lines to either no lines\wide\ medium or narrow.

- Show labels on data points (default:auto), you can set to auto\off.

COLORS AND LEGEND

Colors

You have following options:

- Single color (default)

- By dimension

- By measure

- By expression

If you select by dimension\measure you can select various color schemes.

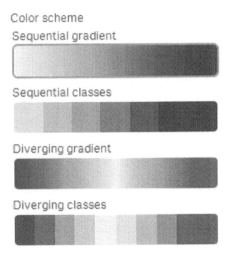

By dimension: Persistent colors, this option is useful if you have drill down dimensions and you want the colors to be the same when you drill down.

Depending on the option you select you also have the option to Show Legends.9999

X-axis:Customer

- Labels and title - Set the option for the x-axis label and title to show either or both.

- Label orientation - horizontal or tilted, tilted is useful if the labels are too long to be shown horizontally.

- Position - Top or Bottom, the default is Bottom which is the norm, x-axis labels on the top looks weird in my opinion but might be useful for very long labels.

Y-axis: Qtr 1 Total

- Labels and title - Set the option for the x-axis label and title to show either or both.

- Position - Left or Right

- Scale - Wide, Medium or Narrow.

In this example a Wide scale creates a y-axis labels of only 0 and 20k whereas the medium scale has the labels 0,5,10 and 15k.

RANGE

The default is auto.

1. Click on the range slider to select Custom.

2. Select either Min, Max or Min/Max.

3. For example select Max and enter a value of 18000.

4. Click done to see the following chart with a custom range up to 18k

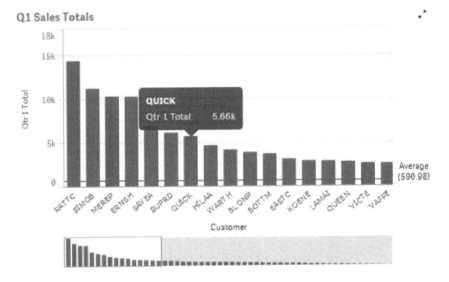

5. Edit the sheet and set the y-axis range back to auto and click save.

RESTRICTING TO THE TOP 5 CUSTOMERS

To restrict your chart to the top 5 customers:

1. Select the Bar chart.

2. Select the Data section in properties pane and expand the Customer dimension.

3. Select a Limitation of 'Fixed number' and Top.

4. Enter 5 in the Limitation text box.

5. Clear the tick from the 'show orders' tick box.

6. Click Save, then click 'Done'.

Your chart should look like the next screenshot:

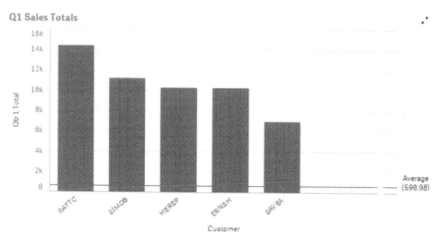

RIGHT CLICK OPTIONS

If you right click on the chart you will have various options such as:

Add to master items

This adds the object to that master items under the visualizations section.

LINE CHART

SETUP THE LINE CHART DATA

1. Open the Charts app

2. Go to the DLE and in the SampleCustomerReports. xls section add the following nested if statement to the LOAD statement.

if("Qtr 1" > 0,'Q1',

if("Qtr 2" > 0,'Q2',

if("Qtr 3" > 0,'Q3',

if("Qtr 4" > 0,'Q4')

))) as Qtr,

if("Qtr 1" > 0,"Qtr 1",

if("Qtr 2" > 0,"Qtr 2",

if("Qtr 3" > 0,"Qtr 3",

if("Qtr 4" > 0,"Qtr 4")

))) as QtrTotal

This statement will return the value "Q1" if the field "Qtr 1" is greater than zero and the same for the other quarters and save the value as the Qtr field.

3. We will use the Qtr field in the line chart for the x-axis.

4. The final section should look like this:

LOAD

Product,

Customer,

"Qtr 1",

"Qtr 2",

"Qtr 3",

"Qtr 4",

//Store the current Quarter

if("Qtr 1" > 0,'Q1',

if("Qtr 2" > 0,'Q2',

if("Qtr 3" > 0,'Q3',

if("Qtr 4" > 0,'Q4')

))) as Qtr,

//Store the current Quarter Total

if("Qtr 1" > 0,"Qtr 1",

if("Qtr 2" > 0,"Qtr 2",

if("Qtr 3" > 0,"Qtr 3",

if("Qtr 4" > 0,"Qtr 4")

))) as QtrTotal

FROM 'lib://data sources/SampleCustomerReports.xls'

(biff, embedded labels, table is [Source Data$]);

5. Click the 'load data' button to reload the app.

Create the Line chart

1. Open the Sales sheet, click the Edit button.

2. Go to the Fields tab in the left pane, right click on the Qtr field, select 'Create dimension'.

3. Click 'Add Dimension'

4. Click Done.

5. Go to the Master Items in the left pane, Right click on the QtrTotal , select 'Create measure'.

6. Change the expression to:

sum(QtrTotal)

7. Click create.

8. Go to the Charts tab.

9. Drag the Line chart object to the sheet in the bottom right corner.

10. Add dimension: Select Qtr

11. Add measure: Select QtrTotal

At the moment the chart will display the total sales for the selections across Q1-Q4.

12. Select the line chart and expand the Data section in the right pane.

13. Click Add Data->Dimension and select customer.

14. Click on appearance, Colors and legend and change the 'Show legend' to auto.

15. Click done and select some customers such as the ones in the next screenshot:

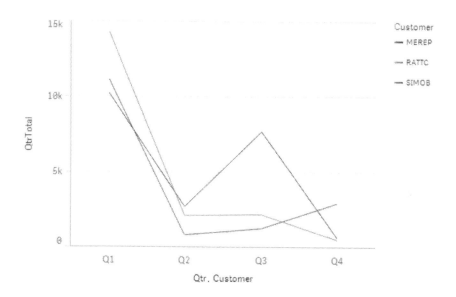

16. Click Save.

Completed app: Charts and Tables\Line Chart\Charts-line1.qvf

PIE CHART

1. In the Charts App open the Sales Sheet and click Edit.

2. Right click on the 'Quarterly Sales Figures' table and select 'Add to master items'.

3. Click Add, this will add this table to the visualization section of the master items.

4. Click the Sheets dropdown list next to the 'Done' button in the top right hand corner.

5. Click 'Create new sheet'.

6. Enter a sheet called 'Dashboard' and press enter.

7. Click on the 'Dashboard' sheet icon

8. Drag a pie chart icon to the sheet.

9. Select a Dimension of Product and Measure of 'QtrTotal'.

10. Click on the title and change it to: 'Product Sales'.

NOTE: Pie charts are only allowed 1 dimension and 1 measure.

The Dimension and measures are similar to the bar\line chart with the ability to set a limitation or Show\Hide the OTHERS dimension.

Measures have the same number formatting options as other chart types.

Pie Chart – Appearance

Presentation

Pie chart or a donut shapes are available.

Value labels

These can be Share (percentage value) or the Values (actual value).

The colors and legend are the same as the other chart types.

11. Click done and save.

12. Select the Global Search button.

13. Search for a customer such as RATTC to see the pie chart change as the image below:

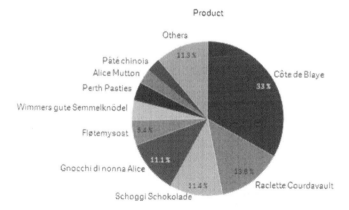

Completed App:

Charts and Tables\Pie Chart\Charts-pie1.qvf

CHART EXPRESSIONS

Chart Expressions are used to calculate the values plotted on the y-axis.

In previous examples we have already created expressions to Sum the total values for a quarter.

We have also create calculated fields in the loadscript using the if statement.

Starting App:

Charts and Tables\Chart Expressions\Charts-Start_Expr. qvf

1. Open the Charts App and select the Dashboard sheet.

2. Drag and drop the 'Text and Image' object to the sheet.

3. Type the following text into the box:

Average Q1 Sales

4. Drag and drop another 'Text and Image' object to the sheet.

5. Click on the Data section in the properties pane, then click 'Add measure'.

6. Enter the following expression which will display the average Q1 sales.

=avg("Qtr 1")

7. Set the number formatting to money.

8. Click the 'fx' button to open the expression editor.

9. Click the dropdownlist where it says 'no aggregation' to see some of the ways you can aggregate measure fields.

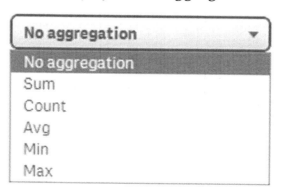

10. Select cancel.

11. Double click the text object with the measure =avg("Qtr 1").

12. A menu we be displayed to format the text. Select a Font size of 'L' for Large text.

13. Select the 'Average Q1 Sales' text and the text with the average measure and select the option to center the text.

14. Click Done to view the text you have added:

Dashboard

Average Q1 Sales

£590.98

15. Click the Edit button on the Dashboard sheet.

16. Select the 'Product Sales' pie chart.

17. Expand the measures in the right pane.

18. Click the x next to the QtrTotal measure to delete it.

19. Click add measure and enter the expression:

   =avg(QtrTotal)

20. Expand the Dimensions section.

21. Expand the product dimension and notice the limitation is set to 10, reduce this to 5.

22. The chart now displays the Average Sales for Q1 for the Top 5 Products.

NOTE: When using logical functions in Qlik Sense such as IsNum() or IsNull() , -1 is returned if the function is true and 0 for false.

Completed App:

Charts and Tables\Chart Expressions\Charts-after expr. qvf

CALCULATED DIMENSION

Calculated Dimensions allow the user to select dimensions based on an expression.

Within Qlik Sense you can create Calculated Dimensions in the Master Items section using functions instead of just selecting fields.

1. For example if you go to the Master Items, Click the Product dimension, select edit.

2. Select the 'fx' option to open the expression editor, click ok to close the warning.

3. Change the expression to:

=Upper(Product)

4. Add a name of 'Product'.

5. Click Save.

6. Click Done and view the results. Notice the Others dimension is not all in upper case. The others dimension label can be changed in the chart properties if required:

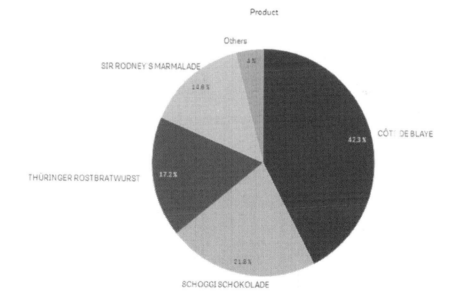

SYNTHETIC DIMENSION FUNCTIONS

In this example we are going to use the ValueList function to create a list of dimensions.

We are going to display the following dimensions:

2012-Q1 and 2012-Q2

These dimensions represent the sum of quarter 1 or quarter 2 sales for the year 2012.

NOTE: These dimensions do not exist in the data.

1. Open the Charts App.

2. Select the Dashboard sheet and click Edit.

3. Select Master Items in the left pane.

4. Expand the Dimension section and click 'Create new'.

5. Open the expression editor by click 'fx'.

Add the expression:

=ValueList('2012-Q1','2012-Q2')

6. Click Apply

7. Add a name of '2012 Q1-Q2'

8. Click Add Dimension, then click Done.

9. Go to the Charts tab in the left pane and drag a bar chart just above the pie chart.

10. Click Data->Add data->Dimension in the properties pane and select the dimension '2012 Q1-Q2' that you just created.

11. Next in the right pane expand the Data section and click Add data->measure.

12. Open the expression editor(fx) and add the following expression:

if(ValueList('2012-Q1','2012-Q2')='2012-Q1',Sum([Qtr 1]),

(

if(ValueList('2012-Q1','2012-Q2')='2012-Q2',Sum([Qtr 2]))

)

)

The format of the IF statement is:

IF(<test something>, <test is TRUE>,<test is FALSE>)

In this example the test we are doing is if the dimension used is either:

'2012-Q1' or '2012-Q2'.

The <test is TRUE> part of the first if statement totals the sales for Qtr 1. The second if statement is nested in the <test is FALSE> part of the first if statement.

13. Click the Apply button.

14. Change the Label field of the measure to:

Sales Total

15. Click on the bar char title and change it to :

Sales 2012 Q1-Q2

16. Click Save and then Done to view your changes that should look like the following chart:

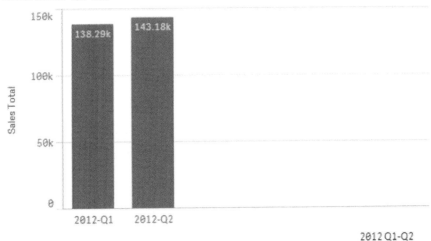

Sales 2012 Q1-Q2

Product Sales

Completed App:

Charts and Tables\Chart Expressions\Charts-afterValueList.qvf

CHART GROUPS

DRILL-DOWN GROUP

This enables you to drill down into the chart for example: Year->Month->Day or Customer->Product.

In this example we are going to setup a drill down group from Customer->Product.

1. Open the Charts App.

2. Select the Sales sheet and click Edit.

3. Go to the Master Items section in the left pane.

4. Click the Dimensions option then click 'Create new'.

Create new dimensions

◯ Single　　◉ Drill-down

5. Select the Drill-down

6. Select the field Customer then Product

7. Enter a name for the new dimension as shown:

Customer->product

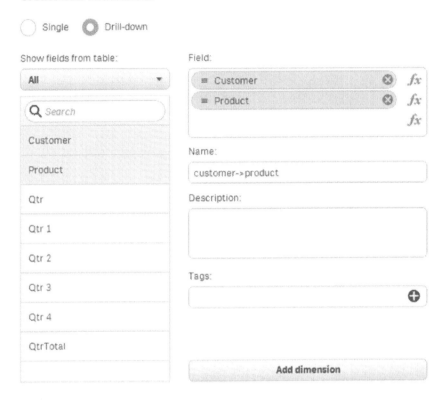

8. Click Add Dimension.

9. Click Done.

You will see the drill-down dimension has a different icon in the master items:

⤵☰ customer->product

10. Select the 'Q1 Sales Totals' bar chart.

11. Expand the Data section in the right pane.

12. Expand the Customer Dimension and click the Delete button on the Customer dimension to remove it from the chart.

13. In the Data section click on 'Add data ->Dimension' and select your customer-product dimension.

14. Click Done and Save.

15. Select one Customer such as RATTC on the x axes of the bar chart.

Notice that the chart drills down into the products for that customer.

Also note that the label of the x axes changes from Customer to Customer->Product.

You can go back to seeing all customers by either removing the selection of the Customer or clicking the Customer part of the 'Customer->Product' x axes label.

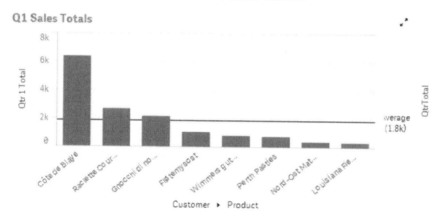

Completed App:

Charts and Tables\Chart Groups\Charts-after-drilldown. qvf

CHANGE CHARTS

You can change chart types by dragging a different chart object over a chart object that has already been created.

For example:

1. Open an app with a bar chart such as 'My first app'.

2. Edit the sheet with the bar chart.

3. From the Charts tab drag the line chart object over the bar chart while holding down the left mouse button.

4. The following menu should appear when you let go of the line chart object:

Replace with new Line chart

Convert to Line chart

Cancel

5. Select the 'Convert to Line chart' to use the same settings.

If you select 'Replace with a new Line chart' you will have to setup the dimensions and measures again.

6. You can repeat this process with a bar chart object over the line chart to return to the bar chart you had before.

PART 5

DEVELOPMENT TIPS

OVERVIEW

In this part we will introduce some tips to help with your Qlik Sense development including:

- How to migrate documents from QlikView to Qlik Sense.

- How to work on apps located in other folders rather than the default Apps folder.

- How to change the app image displayed on the desktop hub.

- Finally we will cover some useful design tips when creating your Qlik Sense apps.

QLIKVIEW TO QLIK SENSE MIGRATION

If you have some QlikView apps you wish to migrate to qlik sense the good news is that you can migrate the data model ie: the load script very easily.

The bad news is that you will have to create the user interface from scratch.

To migrate a qlikview document to a qlik sense app simply:

1. Copy your qvw file into the following path:

C:\Users\<username>\Documents\Qlik\Sense\Apps

2. Open the Qlik Sense Desktop and you will see your app:

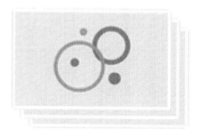

spending (qvw)

3. Alternatively you can drag and drop the qvw to he Qlik Sense Desktop.

4. When you go to the DLE and click the 'load data' button the qvw file will be renamed with an extension of backup

Ie: spending.qvw.backup and a new qvf file will be created in this example called spending.qvf.

5. Before you try to reload the file no qvf will automatically be created.

6. Go to the desktop hub and press F5 to refresh and notice that the title of the app no longer has '(qvw)':

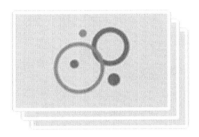

spending

Also remember to check any paths to files such as spreadsheets before trying to reload your data after you have copied your file to the App folder.

SECTION ACCESS AND MIGRATION

Because Qlik Sense uses a different method for security than QlikView you will need to remove any section access security from your document before you try to migrate it.

If you try to open a qvw with section access in qlik sense you will get the following error:

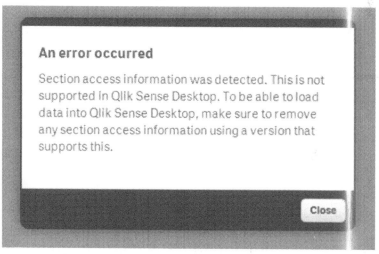

An error occurred

Section access information was detected. This is not supported in Qlik Sense Desktop. To be able to load data into Qlik Sense Desktop, make sure to remove any section access information using a version that supports this.

Close

NOTE: QlikView documents that I could not open with QlikView could be copied to the Qlik Sense Apps folder and migrated to Qlik Sense without any problem. The migration assumes you have access to the data source to reload the document and that there is no section access in the original QlikView document.

MEMORY STICK DEVELOPMENT

One of the reasons that I currently think the Qlik Sense is great is that they have removed the limitation that was in QlikView Personal Edition where you can only open QlikView documents created with that copy of QlikView Personal Edition (QVPE).

This has been removed so there are no limitations between different installations of Qlik Sense Desktop.

The application (QVF) files are located in:

C:\Users\<username>\Documents\Qlik\Sense\Apps.

Within this folder you can create subfolders for your apps and they will still be displayed in the desktop hub.

LINKS TO OTHER FOLDERS

One useful technique is to create a link to a folder within the Apps folder.

This means you can store you applications elsewhere and still access them through the Qlik Sense Desktop as if they were copied into the Apps folder.

For example:

If your Apps were stored in the following folder: E:\ MyApps

1. You would open a Command Prompt window by either clicking the start button and then typing cmd then enter or running the application from Start->All programs->accessories->Command Prompt.

Once the command prompt is open type the following:

cd C:\Users\<username>\Documents\Qlik\Sense\Apps

<username> = the username you are logged into the computer.

2. Enter the following command:

mklink /D MyApps E\MyApps

3. This will return:

symbolic link created for MyApps <<===>> E\MyApps

4. Enter: dir

You will see the directory is listed as follows: Showing that is linked to E:\MyApps.

<SYMLINKD> MyApps [E\MyApps]

5. Now any file you put in E:\MyApps can be accessed through the directory

C:\Users\<username>\Documents\Qlik\Sense\Apps\MyApps

If the files in the E:\MyApps folder are .qvf files the Qlik Sense Desktop will be able to use them.

Possible reasons for doing this is that you might want to keep your apps on a server that is backed up on a regular basis rather or on a memory stick.

NOTE: If you delete the folder you have created with the mklink command it will not delete the source folder but always create a backup just in case of any problems. Better safe than sorry.

APP ICONS

When you start to create several apps on the Qlik Sense Desktop your Desktop hub can start to look quite busy.

One way to improve the look of your apps and make them easier to find is to add an icon to the app.

CREATE YOUR IMAGE

You can create an image for app using any drawing application or select an image you have already.

Personally I like using a website called www.canva.com for creating images or paint.net.

If you are creating your own image try creating one that has a width =380px and height = 236px.

COPY TO QLIK SENSE

Once you have created your image copy it to

C:\Users\<username>\Documents\Qlik\Sense\Content\Default

Where <username> is the username that you have logged into the computer as.

Images you add to this folder can also be used with the 'text & images' object when developing sheets.

SET APP IMAGE IN QLIK SENSE

1. From the desktop hub press F5 to refresh the page. Click the edit button again.

2. Click on the camera icon and select your image.

3. Click apply.

4. Click the edit button again to save the changes.

5. Click Save.

6. Press F5 on the Desktop hub to refresh the page and you should now see the app thumbnail image.

Charts

7. Go to the desktop hub and select the 'Charts' app.

8. Click the edit icon button

If you cannot see the edit icon click on the info button:

Adding app images is useful to highlight the most important apps on your desktop so you can find them quickly without having to search.

USER INTERFACE DESIGN

Improving the design and usability of dashboards such as Qlik Sense documents

In my experience once you consistently use design rules in the development of your Qlik Sense app you will find that not only will you be able to develop your apps faster but the users will be happier with your documents as they will know what to expect.

The truth of the matter is that users don't really like change. Most people can and do live with things that have been designed poorly.

Part of what makes a well-designed app is that users come to expect where certain elements should be such as filter panes.

In this chapter I will describe the most important design techniques to keep in mind when creating your Qlik Sense apps.

Many of these techniques can equally be applied to other reporting software and are not unique to Qlik Sense.

One thing to keep in mind is that good design can be quite subjective and everyone will have their own preferences.

This is especially true when it comes to fonts and colors used in documents.

QLIK DESIGN

Design techniques are all about creating consistency.

The ability to create consistency in your Qlik Sense app

and also between Qlik Sense apps is extremely important.

Users do not like to figure out how to use a Qlik Sense app because the same functions are presented differently in different apps.

If you moving from QlikView to Qlik Sense you will appreciate the global selector (top right hand corner of the sheet) :

The global selector allows the user to select dimensions or fields in the app. In Qlik Sense the current selectors are always displayed at the top of the sheet.

Having a set position for the current selections removes the problem of where to place the current selections object during development that was present in QlikView.

If you follow a set of rules when creating your apps you will find that consistency follows.

How difficult it is to apply design rules will affect how long you spend on the design aspects of your Qlik Sense development.

Creating templates the standard document layout and basic of design of objects can make the task of creating the initial design of Qlik Sense apps easier.

User Interface consistency - For example keeping captions looking the same, consistent colours used.

Data model consistency – For example naming of fields especially key fields.

Give user friendly names to fields that will be used for selection in the user interface, the reason for this is that they name of the field in the data model is what will be displayed in the 'Current Selections'.

Assigning friendly names to fields is even more important if you wish to create a self-service environment where users are confident of creating charts and tables themselves.

Next are a list of techniques to create consistency and also simplify the development process.

Keep the designs as simple as possible

Try not to confuse users with chart types they are not familiar with such as treemaps charts.

Think about Colors – Do you have color bind users?

For color blind users - use different shades of the same color.

Use muted pastally colors, use bright colors to draw attention to something like an error.

SCREEN LAYOUT

Top left corner - place the most important object - This might the ideal location for an important chart or KPI (Key Performance Indicator).

Give most space to most important information.

For example try keeping charts of equal importance to the same size.

If the legends on the X axis are too long you might want to set the legend to a tilted or changing the chart to a horizontal bar chart.

Set the x axis label by selecting the bar chart, expand Appearance, expand X-axis section and change the Label orientation to tilted.

Set to a horizontal chart by selecting the bar chart, expand Appearance->Presentation and selecting the horizontal option.

DAR APP DEVELOPMENT

The DAR methodology for developing QlikView\Qlik Sense apps suggests you break your app into the following types of sheets:

- Dashboard
- Analysis
- Reports

The reason for this is that users will have differing requirements of what information they require from an app.

DASHBOARD

This is where the key KPIs (Key Performance Indicators) will be placed.

The KPIs give an overall picture of the data in the app and indicate if there are any problems that need investigating.

ANALYSIS

This is where you can add more analysis of the data in your app such as tables and various charts and graphs that are not required for the higher level view in the dashboard sheet.

Reports

Put the detail on another sheet

Have selections and overviews of the data on one sheet with the detail level on a separate sheet.

Having access to the data used in the app is useful when someone queries the data used in a kpi or wants to export the data to Excel to perform their own analysis.

Remove unnecessary elements.

This might see obvious but is sometimes overlooked in an effort to try give the end user everything they might require.

MASTER ITEMS

If you are going to use a table in more than 1 sheet it s worth while adding the object to the master items visualization section.

You can do this when you are editing the document by right click on the object and selecting 'add to master items'.

Then on other sheets you can drag and drop the object from the master items visualization section to the sheet.

Add common Dimensions \ Measures to the master items. This will save time when creating new sheets and also make it easier for your users to create their own sheets and objects which is the aim of self-service visualization and self-service analytics.

NOTE: Once the object is added to the master items it can only be changed through the master items, by clicking on the object and selecting edit. Any changes will update all copies of the object.

If you select an object in the master items visualization section you will see the following message in the right pane where the properties for the object would normally be displayed:

Linked visualization
A linked visualization cannot be edited.

SCRIPT LIBRARY

Create a library of useful scripts.For example:

Scripts to implement incremental qvds.

Create a master calendar table to have common selections of dates for each sheet.

CHART TYPES

Bar Charts

The most common chart type is the bar chart.

Use a single color for the bar color as using multi-colored bars does not normally add anything useful.

Line Charts

Line charts are used to represent values that are changing over time for example time, date or some period of time.

For example think of computer performance data where the amount of memory used is plotted over time in the Windows Task Manager or the profits of a company might be plotted over time to see how well the company is performing.

Pie Charts

The problem with pie charts is that it is difficult to compare areas effectively.

Especially if many dimensions need to be displayed in more than one pie chart.

If possible instead of a pie chart you could use a bar chart.

Useful Design Tools

For finding out which colors that go together

http://jiminy.medialab.sciences-po.fr/tools/palettes

https://kuler.adobe.com

http://www.colorschemer.com/colorpix_info.php

An Open Source vector graphics editor – very useful for creating images

http://inkscape.org/

Creating images online

www.canva.com

Looking for different fonts

http://www.fontsquirrel.com/

http://www.colorschemer.com/colorpix_info.php

SUMMARY

Think about the users - talk to users

Think of the end users – current and future users (and developers) - Add a full description of the App.

If you would like to look into design in more depth I would suggest starting with the following book by Stephen Few:

Information Dashboard Design: The Effective Visual Communication of Data by Stephen Few

Personally I find having a set of techniques that I can remember and are therefore more likely to use more useful.

Whereas reading books that are focused on the design of dashboards will certainly give an insight into questions such as why some chart types are not useful. You might not remember all the design tips months after reading them.

My advice is to start using a few techniques on a regular basis until they become second nature and progress from there.

SCRIPTS AND DEBUG

When you have been developing with Qlik Sense for some time you will begin to notice that certain scripts and variables are used again and again.

Rather than copying code it is best practice to have the script in one place and just include the code in the apps as required.

A good example is a table that converts the numeric value of the month to the short name:

Calendar:

LOAD * INLINE [

MONTH, MONTHNAME

1, Jan

2, Feb

3, Mar

4, Apr

5, May

6, Jun

7, Jul

8, Aug

9, Sep

10, Oct

11, Nov

12, Dec

];

To include the file using the following format

$(include='<filename>');

For example if the file is in the same folder as the app use:

$(include='monthtable.txt');

Use could also use a connection to a folder data source, ie: if the file was in the 'data sources' folder :

$(include='lib://data sources/monthtable.txt');

If the file that you want to include does not exist the script will not fail.

To make sure that the script fails it the file does not exist change the include to must_include as shown:

$(must_include='lib://data sources/monthtable.txt');

TRACE COMMAND

It is also useful to add trace commands especially in long scripts and in external script files.

The Trace command is used to output the value of variables and message while the script it loading.

For example:

TRACE Loading the monthnum to monthname table;

Or to display the number of rows in a table:

LET rowcount = noofrows('mytable');

TRACE Rows = $(rowcount);

Where the noofrows function function returns the row count for table 'mytable' into the variable rowcount.

LOGS

In the following folder you will find detailed logs for each app and qliksense desktop.

C:\Users\<username>\Documents\Qlik\Sense\Log

The logs for the individual apps are useful for getting more information about the last time the app was reloaded.

SUBROUTINES

To make your code even more reusable you can create block of code that you can reuse again and again and change certain variables.

For example: you might want to create a subroutine for creating qvd's and just pass the table name you wish to read.

In this example we will show a simple subroutine that takes 1 parameter called somevalue.

In the subroutine we will simply output the value of the parameter using the trace command.

sub myfirstsub(somevalue)

trace Parameter value = $(somevalue);

end sub

Sub is short for subroutine, followed by the subroutine name, then any parameter in brackets (the parameters are optional).

You enclose the code in the sub..end sub keywords.

CALLING THE SUBROUTINE

For example:

call myfirstsub(5);

call myfirstsub(6);

call myfirstsub(7);

Output from the subroutine:

Parameter value = 5

Parameter value = 6

Parameter value = 7

No parameter sub

To call a subroutine without parameters you don't even have to include the brackets:

sub anothersub

trace no parameters here;

end sub

CALLING THE NO PARAMETER SUBROUTINE

For example:

call anothersub;

Using subroutines can save you a lot of time when developing your qlik sense apps.

When you start to see yourself either having to copy the same type of code to several apps it is a clear sign that you could start using script files to store subroutines and scripts such variables and inline tables to speed up your development.

LOADSCRIPT TIPS

NULLS

There are various ways in which you can deal with Nulls in QlikSense.

1. Change null values in the loadscript using an if statement and the isNull function which returns -1 for true\0 for false

Ie: In the load statement you could use:

If(isNull(Country)=-1,'No Country',Country) as Country

If the Country field is null this expression will set the Country field to 'No Country' otherwise the value in the Country field will be used.

2. NullDisplay - ODBC

You can set the NullDisplay variable in the loadscript to determine the value of ODBC null values, for example:

Set NullDisplay = 'NULL';

3. NullInterpret - Files

The NullInterpret is used to define which values should be regarded as null in Excel, text or inline tables:

For example to return NULL for blanks in Excel:

Set NullInterpret='';

For example to return NULL for blanks in text files:

Set NullInterpret=' ';

4. NullAsValue

For the specified fields set any NULL values to the NullValue variable, for example:

NullAsValue FieldA, FieldB;

Set NullValue ='None Found';

5. NullCount

To count the number of nulls in a field: NullCount(fieldname)

BOOKMARKS

Sometimes you make certain selections on your qlik sense app and would like to use the same selections the next time that you open the qlik sense app. This can be done using bookmarks.

Starting App:

Advanced\Set Analysis\Charts - before - sa.qvf

1. Open the Charts app (Charts - before - sa.qvf)

2. Open the Sales sheet and select a Customer and Product.

3. Click the bookmarks icon:

4. Click 'Create new bookmark'.

5. Enter a title for the bookmark or keep the title that is generated by the sheetname and selections made, for example:

Sales - Customer (1), =Upper(Product) (1)

If you selected just one customer the default bookmark title might be:

Dashboard - Customer ("ALFKI")

6. To delete a bookmark just right click on the bookmark in the list of bookmarks and select delete option.

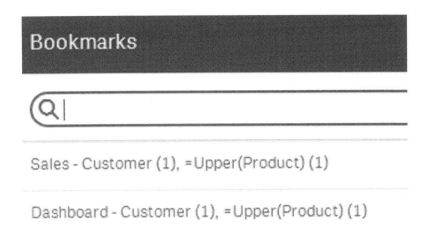

7. You can also access the bookmarks from the Navigation->'app overview' by selecting the bookmark icon on the left hand side of the screen as shown.

Opening bookmarks from the app overview opens the sheet that was active when the bookmark was created and sets the selections for the bookmark.

BINARY STATEMENT

Use the binary statement to load the data from an existing qlik sense app.

Only one binary statement allowed in your qlik sense app.

Binary statement can load multiple tables whereas QVDs load only one table at a time.

1. Create a new app called 'Binary Test', go to the DLE.

2. Enter the following command will be entered at the top of the load script.

BINARY Executive Dashboard.qvf;

3. Click the load data button and then go to the DMV to check the data from the 'Executive Dashboard' app has been loaded into your new app.

4. Using the BINARY command is useful when you need to experiment with new User Interface objects but want to do it in another document without any sheet.

EXPORT DATA TO EXCEL

Starting app:

My first qlik sense app\My first app-completed.qvf

1. With qlik sense open, browse to the web interface:

http://localhost:4848/hub

2. Open the app My first app-completed.

3. Open the sheet 'My new sheet', and right click on the chart and select the '...' button then the 'Export data' button.

4. Click on the link to download the data and it will open in Excel.

5. The same Excel spreadsheet can be found the normal internet download folder for your computer as well as:

C:\Users\<username>\Documents\Qlik\Sense\Exports

PART 6
ADVANCED TOPICS

OVERVIEW

In this final part we will cover some of the more advanced topics such as:

- Advanced sheet objects including gauges, scatter plot and treemap.

- Managing the data model.

- Calendar tables.

- Advanced functions including class, aggr, intervalmatch and dual.

- Using SQL stored procedures.

- Set analysis.

- QVDs to store data read from data sources and incremental loads.

- An introduction to qlik sense extensions.

Before continuing with this part of the book make sure you are comfortable creating the previous examples.

STORYTELLING

Storytelling is a new feature in Qlik Sense that allows the user create snapshots of objects such as tables and charts from the sheet that can be used later to create a slideshow.

The user can also add whole sheets to the slideshow and return to the sheets during the slideshow if required.

This storytelling feature is a very useful tool but whether or not users can be encouraged to move away from their Microsoft Powerpoint slides is yet to be seen.

From an IT perspective I think that the storytelling feature would be useful to include stories with new documents to explain more about the data and any calculations that might not be obvious to the user.

SNAPSHOTS

Snapshots are simply screenshots of sheet objects that you will use to build the slides of your story later on.

1. Make the selections you wish to the sheet while you are using the app (ie: not editing).

2. Click on the menu next to the navigation, if you hover over the button it will just say 'Menu':

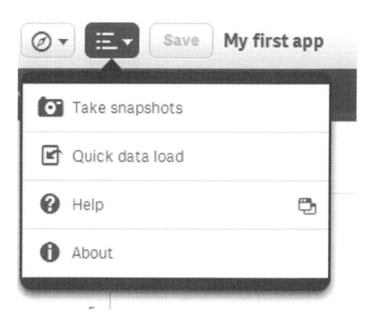

3. Select 'Take snapshots'.

You will see orange boxes with dashed lines around the objects on the sheet.

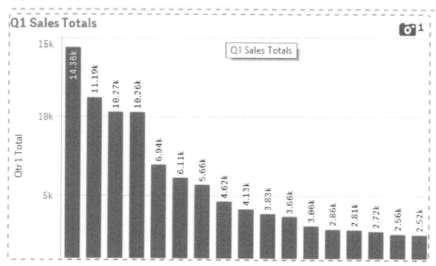

4. Click on each object you wish to save for creating stories later.

5. Then click on the Done button next to the menu when you have finished.

DATA STORYTELLING

6. Click on the data storytelling button from within a sheet or from the app overview.

7. Click create new story.

8. Give the story a title such as 'My first story' or something more meaningful.

9. Click on the new story icon:

My first story

10. The story editor should be displayed.

11. You can use the + button on the left pane to add new slides and the icons on the right pane to add:

- Snapshots
- Text
- Shapes
- Effects
- Media

12. To add snapshots you simply click the snapshots button the drag the snapshot details to the slide.

In the same way you can add text and shapes.

13. You can make changes to the way the snapshot is displayed by clicking the edit (pencil icon) within the snapshot option.

14. In 'effects' you have the ability to highlight values in the snapshots such as the highest or lowest values. If you drag the 'any value' option you can select which value to highlight from a dropdown list.

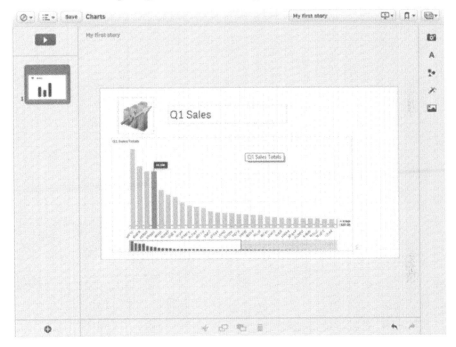

15. You can make your own media available from the media button by copying the image into the following folder:

C:\Users\<username>\Documents\Qlik\Sense\Content\Default

16. You will need to go back to the Desktop Hub and press F5 to refresh application then you can go back into the story and add the image to your slide.

17. Click the Green play button in the top of the left pane to test your story.

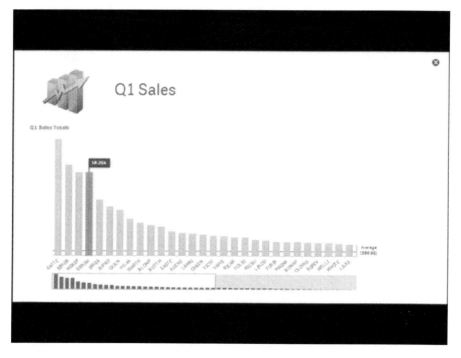

18. Click on the x in the top right corner to go back and click on the + to add a new slide, this time select 'Sheet' and then 'Sales' to add the sales sheet to your story.

19. Select the play button again and this time you will be able to use the left\right arrow keys to move between the slides.

20. Notice that on the slide that contains the Sales sheet you can make selection or even click on the 'go to sheet' button to go back to the sheets.

This ability to dive back into the sheets can be useful if you are giving a presentation and someone queries the underlying data or the discussion evolves in an unforeseen way.

ADVANCED SHEET OBJECTS

Overview

In this section we will be covering the more advanced and arguably more interesting aspects of the chart object.

When developing Qlik Sense apps most people focus on the bar chart and tables as they are the most common object types.

In this chapter we will cover how to use various sheet objects such as the Combo chart, Gauge, scatter plot and treemap.

Advanced Sample Data Setup

1. Create a new app called Advanced.

2. Drag and drop the file SampleCustomerReports.xls to the app and add the Source Data$ table.

3. Go to the DLE and change the script to make the following:

NOTE: The name of the connection to the file SampleCustomerReports.xls might be different in your case.

(see: Advanced\ Advanced Sheet Objects\ adv sample data setup.txt)

CustomerSales:

crosstable(Quarter,Amount,2)

LOAD

Product,

Customer,

"Qtr 1",

"Qtr 2",

"Qtr 3",

"Qtr 4"

FROM 'lib://data sources/SampleCustomerReports.xls'

(biff, embedded labels, table is [Source Data$]);

LINE CHART

Line charts are commonly used to represent values that are changing over time for example time, date or some period of time.

In this example we are going plot the sales total for one particular company over the 4 quarters.

Line chart example

4. Go to the DLE.

5. First we need to change the loadscript to use the crosstable feature as shown in the next script:

CustomerSales:

crosstable(Quarter,Amount,2)

LOAD

Product,

Customer,

"Qtr 1",

"Qtr 2",

"Qtr 3",

"Qtr 4"

FROM 'lib://data sources/SampleCustomerReports.xls'

(biff, embedded labels, table is [Source Data$]);

6. Click the 'load data' button.

CROSSTABLES

The crosstable option is used to combine data several columns.

The cross table option:

Crosstable(attribute,data, no qualifier fields)

Attribute field - in this case it is Quarter and will be Qtr1-4.

Data - this is set to Amount and is the sales figure.

No Qualifier fields - This is the number of fields to ignore before the Attribute\Data fields.

In this case it is the 2 fields Product and Customer.

7. Once the document is reloaded the current table should have the four fields:

Product,Customer ,Quarter and Amount

Preview of data

Product	Customer	Quarter	Amount
Alice Mutton	ANTON	Qtr 2	702
Alice Mutton	BERGS	Qtr 1	312
Alice Mutton	BOLID	Qtr 4	1170
Alice Mutton	BOTTM	Qtr 1	1170
Alice Mutton	ERNSH	Qtr 1	1123.2
Alice Mutton	ERNSH	Qtr 4	2607.15
Alice Mutton	GODOS	Qtr 2	280.8

Create the line chart

1. Go to the app overview and select the 'My new sheet' sheet.

2. Click the edit button to put the sheet in edit mode.

3. Go to the master items in the left pane and add:

A dimension of Quarter.

A measure using the following expression called 'BERGS Sales':

=sum({<Customer={'BERGS'}>}[Amount])

This expression is used to calculate the total sales amount for the customer BERGS as shown:

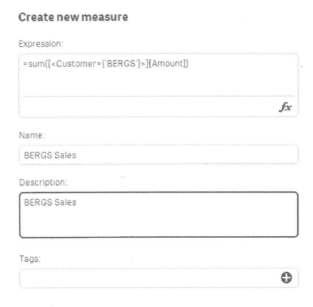

Create new measure

Expression:

```
=sum({<Customer={'BERGS'}>}[Amount])
```

fx

Name:

BERGS Sales

Description:

BERGS Sales

Tags:

4. Drag a line chart to the sheet and select the dimension and measure you have just created.

5. Add a title to the chart by clicking on the title and entering 'BERGS Sales'.

6. Click done and save the sheet. Your line chart should look like the following screenshot:

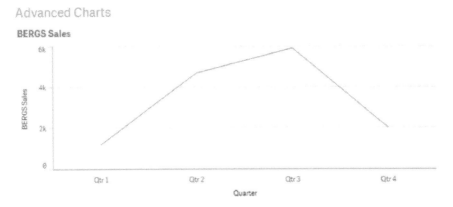

COMPARING TRENDS - MULTIPLE CUSTOMERS

The advantage of using line charts instead of bar charts when plotting data over time is that it is easy to see trends especially when you have multiple values plotted on the same chart.

1. Add the Dimension of Customer to the master items.

2. Add a measure to the master items called 'B customers' using the following expression used to include all customers that start with B:

=sum({<Customer={'B*'}>}[Amount])

3. Create a new line chart using:

Dimensions: Quarter then Customer.

Measure 'B Customers'.

4. Add a title to your chart and turn the legend on in the Appearance->Colors and Legend section of the right pane.

5. Click the Done button to view the result.

Now multiple customers will be displayed, it is easy to see that Customer BERGS is doing very well until it comes to Qtr 4.

See if your chart looks like the following screenshot:

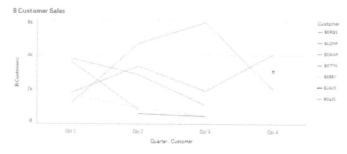

Whereas if you created a bar chart using the same dimensions and measure it is not as easy to see the trends in the sales amounts for the customers between customers as in the line chart.

COMBO CHARTS

Combo charts are simply a combination of a line and bar chart.

The advantage is that we can show one expression as a bar chart and another expression as a line chart.

In this example we will show the average sales for all customers over the quarter as a line chart and the max sales in each quarter as a bar chart.

Starting App:

Advanced\Advanced Sheet Objects\Combo charts\ Advanced-start-combo.qvf

1. Open the Advanced app then Open the 'Advanced Charts' sheet and click edit.

Add the following measures to the Master Items:

Average Sales: avg(Amount)

Max Sale: max(Amount)

Min Sale: min(Amount)

2. Drag a combo chart to the sheet.

3. Add a Dimension of Quarter.

4. Add the following Measures:

Max Sale - Select a Type of 'Line', change axis to 'Secondary axis.

Average Sales - select 'Bars' as the Type.

Min Sale - Select Marker as the type and choose the circle as the marker.

5. In the appearance section -> Colors and Legend -> Set 'Show Legend' to auto.

6. Click the chart title and set to 'Sales Analysis'.

7. Click Done and Save, your chart should look like this:

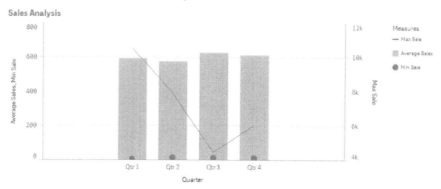

Completed App:

Advanced\Advanced Sheet Objects\Combo charts\ Advanced-combo-completed.qvf

GAUGES

Gauge chart types are used to plot single values against ranges, when you think of gauges think of a speedometer in a car where the current speed of the car is displayed against the minimum and maximum possible speeds.

Another example is:

Total Sales for the month might be plotted against:

Poor Sales 1-10m

Average Sales 11-20m

Excellent Sales 21-100m

Gauges are frequently used on the dashboard sheet of your app in place of where a single text value would have been displayed.

The advantage of the gauges is that the user can tell at a glance if something needs more analysis.

Gauge Example

1. Open the 'Charts' Qlik Sense app.

2. Open the 'Dashboard' sheet and click edit.

3. Drag a Gauge object to the sheet, click add measure and select 'Qtr 1 Total'.

4. Add a Title of 'Qtr 1 Total' to the Gauge.

5. Click on the measure and set Number Formatting to money.

6. In the properties pane on the right of the sheet click on the Appearance->Presentation.

7. Set the max value to 200000.

8. Click on 'Use segments', click 'add limit', Set the limit to 100000, you will notice that the bar above the segment limit it split into 2,click the segment on the left and choose the red color.

9. Click 'add limit' again, Set the limit to 150000.

10. Click on the middle segment and select a yellow color.

11. Click on the end segment and select a green color.

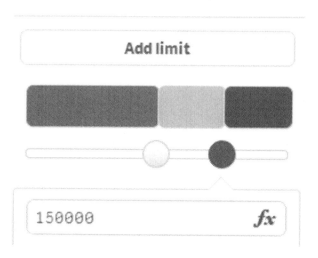

Add limit

150000   *fx*

12. Click Done and Save to get your gauge.

Make some selections to see the gauge update.

The result should look like the image below:

Completed App:

Advanced\Advanced Sheet Objects\Gauges\Charts-after guage.qvf

SCATTER PLOT

The scatter plot is a chart that can display 1 dimension and 2 measures.

Points are plotted using the x (dimension) / y (1st measures) axes but the 2nd measure is used to display the size\color of each point.

The scatter plot is often used to see if there is a relationship between 2 measures (also known as the correlation).

Scatter plot example

1. Open the Advanced App and create a sheet called 'Advanced Analysis', open and edit the sheet.

2. Go to the Master Items and add a measure called 'Q1 Totals' with the expression:

sum({<Quarter={'Qtr 1'}>} Amount)

3. Drag a scatter plot chart to the sheet.

4. Add the Dimension:

Quarter

5. Add the measures:

Average Sales

Q1 Totals

6. You can change the size of the bubble in Appearance->Presentation in the properties pane.

7. You can experiment with the color of the bubble in appearance->color and legend.

The default is 'single color'

Other options are by dimension or by expression.

'By expression' might be useful to highlight another variable by setting the bubble color red if it is over some threshold.

8. Click Done and Save, your chart should look like the following screenshot.

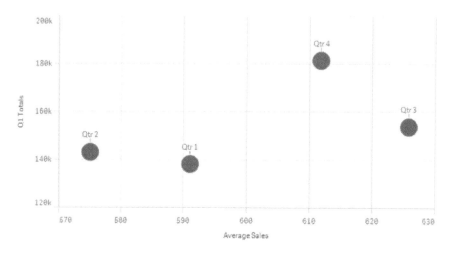

Notice that the 2 measures are plotted on the x and y axes whereas the dimension is the label for each bubble.

9. Edit the sheet, delete the Quarter dimension and add the Customer dimension.

10. Click Done and Save. Your chart should look like the following screenshot:

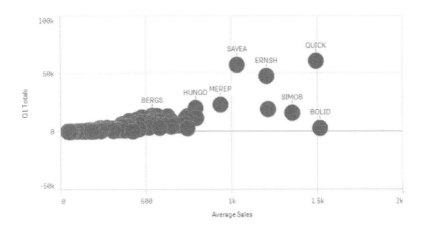

You can see that customer BOLID has the best average sales but did very poorly in Q1.

Whereas customer QUICK did well in the average and Q1 sales.

Completed App:

Advanced\ Advanced Sheet Objects\ Scatter plot\

Advanced-afterscatter.qvf

TREEMAP

Treemaps are used to display hierarchical data using nested rectangles. Each dimension of the data has a rectangle.

The size of the rectangle is proportional to the measure value.

In a treemap you can add one or more dimensions and measures.

The default sort order is by the measure value.

NOTE: Negative values cannot be displayed in a treemap.

Treemap Example

1. Open the Advanced app and edit the Advanced Analysis Sheet.

2. Go to the master items and create a drill down dimension of customer and product as shown:

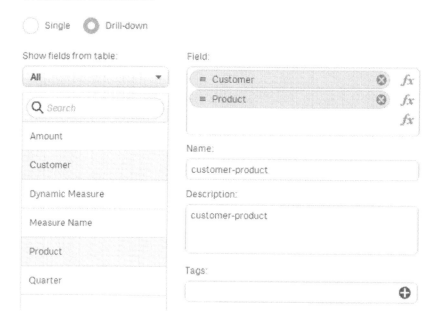

3. Drag the treemap object to the sheet.

4. Add the 'customer-product' dimension.

5. Add the measure 'Average Sales'.

6. Change the change title to 'Average Sales'. Then in the properties pane set Appearance->Presentation->Colors-> to 'By Dimension'.

7. Click 'Done' and then Save to view your treemap and compare to the following treemap:

Average Sales

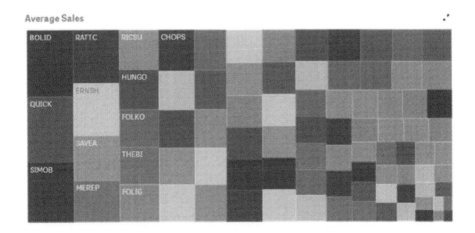

8. Click on Customer RATTC and confirm the selection, to see the treemap change to:

Average Sales

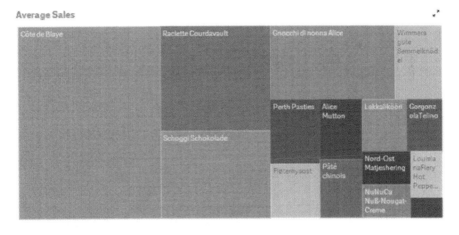

Selecting the customer drills down into the products for that customer.

Completed App:

Advanced\ Advanced Sheet Objects\ Treemap\

Treemap-after-basic.qvf

Multiple Dimensions

1. Edit the Advanced analysis sheet again.

2. Remove the customer-product dimension.

3. Add the dimensions Customer then Quarter.

4. Click Done and then Save to view your treemap:

Now the rectangle is divided into the size of average sales for each quarter:

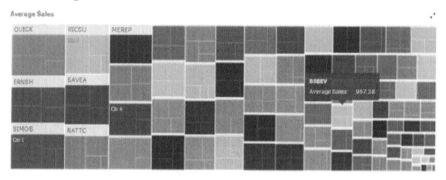

5. Click on Customer RATTC and confirm the selection.

Now the treemap only displays customer RATTC and when you hover over the rectangles the average sales for each quarter is displayed.

Completed App:

Advanced\Advanced Sheet Objects\Treemap\Treemap-after-cust-quarter.qvf

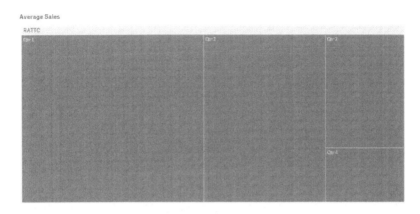

6. Finally edit the treemap again and add the dimension of product.

The dimensions in order should be:

Customer

Quarter

Product

7. Click save and then done.

8. Now when you select customer RATTC you will see that the treemap is divided into Quarters and products.

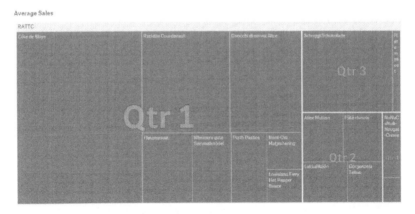

You can then select a Quarter such as qtr 1 as shown in the next screenshot:

Completed App:

Advanced\Advanced Sheet Objects\Treemap\Treemap-after-cust-qtr-product.qvf

Try experimenting with the treemap by setting the color of the rectangles in the treemap properties (right pane) in Appearance->Colors.

Set to Custom and select another option such as 'By measure' and view the result. Here we can see the darker colors highlight the higher measures.

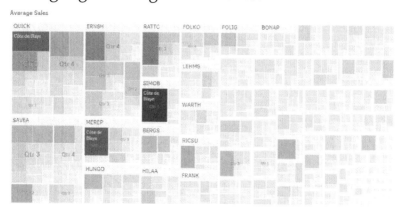

Completed App:

Advanced\Advanced Sheet Objects\Treemap\

Treemap-after by measure.qvf

URL LINKS

Using the 'text & image' object you can create url links, for example to open another website or another app:

1. Drag the 'text & image object' to the sheet.

2. Enter some text and highlight the text ie: google.

3. Click on the url button (the chain icon) and add a url ie: http://google.com

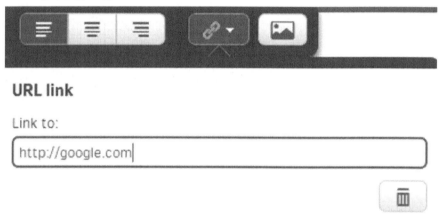

4. Click Done to test the Url:

LINKS TO OTHER APPS

You can even create links to other apps.

To do this you will need to find out the url of the app.

1. Open the desktop hub in a browser:

Http://localhost:4848/hub

2. Click on one of your apps and copy the url to use in a

'text & image' object.

For example: This is the url to the 'My first app' app on my machine:

http://localhost:4848/sense/app/C%3A%5CUsers%5Cu sername%5CDocuments%5CQlik%5CSense%5CApps%5 Ctest2%5CMy%20first%20app

The main use of url links would be to open a url for an app or it you are using qlikview in your company and it the process of migrating some apps to qlik sense you might use the url links to qlikview documents.

MANAGING THE QLIK SENSE DATA MODEL

Only use the data you need.

In Qlik Sense the schema is critical – a selection in Qlik Sense affects the whole schema.

Therefore you need to develop the load script with the end in mind.

Try to keep the complexity in the load scripts and away for the GUI this will improve the performance of your app especially in a working environment.

If the data model is correct it should make the development of the GUI easier.

This is even more important if you have separate design teams that will be using your data.

Also it is more time consuming to copy complex expressions into several sheet objects and the maintenance of changes to those expressions.

If there are some tables\fields that you only require while creating the table or QVD you can drop these after they have been used using the drop command to reduce any data that is not required in the final app, for example:

DROP TABLE tablename

DROP FIELD fieldname

FACT AND DIMENSION TABLES

Fact tables contain the values that the expressions will be

based on. For example a fact table for a dimensional model based on product orders might contain fields such as the amount the order costs and any discounts\taxes.

Whereas the dimension tables would contain values used to select records in the fact table. For example common dimension tables are a calendar dimension table which would allow the selection of months\years, a country dimension table and a sales person dimension table.

Dimension tables connect to the fact table using key fields such as an id field.

One method is to manage and create reusable dimension tables is to create a QVD for each Dimension table. This will be covered later in this section.

STAR SCHEMA

Star schema arranges the dimension tables around a central fact table that contains the measures.

The dimension tables arranged around a central fact table that contains the measures.

Each dimension is only one table.

The dimension tables are used to selections for example a list of customer names.

Whereas the fact table contains the details that will be used in calculations for example order amount details.

SNOWFLAKE SCHEMA

Like Star schema but the dimensions are normalized into several tables. When tables are normalized this means that they have been organized using rules called normal forms in such a way to reduce duplication of data and try to organize the data in a logical fashion.

LINK TABLES

1. Sometimes called dimensional link tables.

2. Link tables are commonly used to solve problems such as:

a. To remove Circular references \ synthetic keys and tidy your data model.

b. Multiple fact tables – the usual example is when comparing budget and actual data which you wish to keep the fact tables separate.

c. To create links between tables where links do not already exist. For example by combining 2 fields and using the autonumber function to create a key. Use the autonumber function to create keys has the added benefit of using less memory, for example:

Load   Autonumber(ProductID&'-'&OrderID   )   as %ProdOrderKey

ProductID,

OrderID

From sometable;

Using linked tables are an alternative to concatenating two tables one and having a field to indicate which table the record originally belonged to.

To create a Link Table to 2 fact tables you need to:

1. Concatenate keys used to link to the fact and dimension tables into 1 table.

2. All tables should have a unique key.

3. Use Autonumber to save space on long keys.

4. Break any existing links between tables so that you don't get synthetic keys or circular references by renaming fields or using qualify.

Link Table Example

For this example we will alter a Qlik Sense app that is being used to track the users spending in various categories such as Food and Coffee to add budgets for each Category\ Month.

1. Create a new App called 'Spending'.

2. Drag the spreadsheet qv_spending_updated.xls to the app.

Load the sheets Jan and Budget as shown:

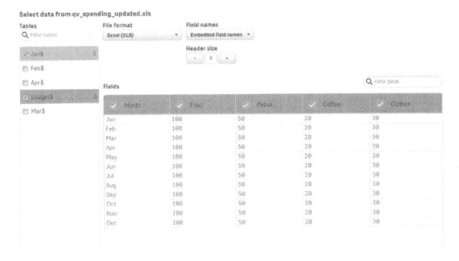

3. The budget data is in a sheet called budget, for example:

Month	Food	Petrol	Coffee	Clothes
Jan	100	50	20	30
Feb	100	50	20	30
Mar	100	50	20	30

4. The initial load will contain the script:

LOAD

"Date",

Food,

Petrol,

Coffee,

Clothes

FROM 'lib://data sources/qv_spending_updated.xls'

(biff, embedded labels, table is Jan$);

LOAD

"Month",

Food,

Petrol,

Coffee,

Clothes

FROM 'lib://data sources/qv_spending_updated.xls'

(biff, embedded labels, table is budget$);

5. Add the table names as track_spending and budget.

6. Next we will alter the load of the Jan sheet to loop around all the spending sheets.

Surround the load statement for the spending sheet in a for each...next loop as shown:

For Each *Sheetname* in 'Jan$','Feb$','Mar$'

<LOAD statement for spending sheets>

Next

7. Add a CrossTable command before the LOAD statements for the spending sheet and budget sheets:

CrossTable(Category, Amount)

8. Replace Jan$ in the LOAD statement with the variable that contains the sheet names:

$(Sheetname)

9. Add the following loadscript:

(see Advanced\Managing the Qlik Sense Data Model\ spending load_synthetic.txt)

For Each Sheetname in 'Jan$','Feb$','Mar$'

track_spending:

CrossTable(Category, Amount)

LOAD

"Date",

Food,

Petrol,

Coffee,

Clothes

FROM 'lib://data sources/qv_spending_updated.xls'

(biff, embedded labels, table is $(Sheetname));

Next

budget:

CrossTable(Category, Amount)

LOAD

"Month",

Food,

Petrol,

Coffee,

Clothes

FROM 'lib://data sources/qv_spending_updated.xls'

(biff, embedded labels, table is budget$);

10. The first loop in the script loads all the monthly spending data whereas the second part loads the budget data.

11. This gives a synthetic key - multiple keys between the 2 tables.

Next we will create a link table to fix this synthetic key problem.

CREATE DIMENSIONS AND LINK TABLE

Alter the loadscript to create a link table to match the script below.

By creating the dimension tables which are used for selections, the link table and the fact tables you will remove the synthetic keys from the data model.

In the DLE of the Spending app: Add a section called Maps and insert the following script:

// This mapping table is used to convert the numeric value of the month into the short string

// for the month

MonthMap:

MAPPING

LOAD * INLINE [

Num, Name

1, Jan

2, Feb

3, Mar

4, Apr

5, May

6, Jun

7, Jul

8, Aug

9, Sep

10, Oct

11, Nov

12, Dec

];

2. Create a Section called 'Dimensions' and add the following script to create the dimensions:

//Create the Dimension Tables

dim_category:

LOAD distinct Category

Resident track_spending;

LOAD Category

Resident budget

WHERE NOT Exists(Category);

//Month Dimension - in this example we are loading the months from the track_spending table and the budget table

dim_month:

NoConcatenate LOAD distinct

ApplyMap('MonthMap', month(Date)) as Month

Resident track_spending;

LOAD Month

Resident budget;

3. Add a section called 'Key tables' and add the following:

//KEY: Budget\Actual - Month - Date - Category

link_table:

```
LOAD distinct

Category

,Month

,'Budget' & '-' &Month& '-' & '$(ANY)' & '-' &Category as
%link_key

Resident budget;

LOAD distinct

Category

,ApplyMap('MonthMap', month(Date)) as Month

,'Actual' & '-' & '$(ANY)' & '-' &month(Date)& '-'
&Category as %link_key

Resident track_spending;

//Fact tables

fact_budget:

LOAD

Amount

,'Budget' & '-' &Month& '-' & '$(ANY)' & '-' &Category as
%link_key

,'Budget' as Type

Resident budget;

LOAD

Amount

,'Actual' & '-' & '$(ANY)' & '-' &month(Date)& '-'
&Category as %link_key
```

,'Actual' as Type

Resident track_spending;

//Remove the original tables

DROP TABLE track_spending;

DROP TABLE budget;

4. Click 'load data', notice that they is no synthetic key.

Go to the DMV to view the data model.

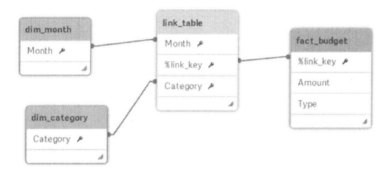

5. Create a new sheet called 'Detail'.

6. Create the following Dimensions in the master items:

Category

Month

Type

7. Create the following Measures in the master items:

'Spent Amount' as :

sum({<Type={'Actual'} >}Amount)

'Budget Amount' as :

sum({<Type={'Budget '} >}Amount)

8. Now you can create a simple table to display the data in the dimension and fact tables and add the category and month fields as filter panes for selection as shown in the screenshot.

Here I created a table with the Category, Spent Amount and Budget Amount columns and filter panes for Category and Month.

Actual v Budget Spending

Category	Spent Amount	Budget Amount
Totals	1105.69	2400
Clothes	169.99	360
Coffee	195.7	240
Food	280	1200
Petrol	460	600

Q **Month**

Apr

Aug

Dec

Feb

Jan

Jul

Jun

Mar

Q **Category**

Clothes

Coffee

Food

Petrol

Completed App:

Advanced\Managing the Qlik Sense Data Model\ Spending-after link example.qvf

JOINING TABLES

WHAT ARE TABLE JOINS?

Table joins allow you to combine columns of data from different tables.

Table joins check if there are rows that match between 2 tables based on matching field names.

As normal in Qlik Sense you have to make sure you only have 1 field in common in both tables otherwise you will get synthetic tables.

If you have written SQL statements before you will have almost certain come across table joins and will have no problem in understanding joins in Qlik Sense.

Remember:

Joins add columns whereas concatenation adds rows.

WHY USE JOINS?

The most common reason to use SQL joins is to reduce the number of tables in your data model.

Alternatives to using joins in Qlik Sense are:

1. ApplyMap and Mapping tables to add a field to the table.

2. Joining the tables in the SQL SELECT statement or a SQL stored procedure.

JOIN TYPES

Default is a full outer join.

To demonstrate how the different join options work we will used the following inline tables:

1. Create an app called 'Joins'.

2. Create a section in the DLE called 'join data' add the following inline tables:

(Advanced\Managing the Qlik Sense Data Model\join_tables.txt)

Starting App:

Advanced\Managing the Qlik Sense Data Model\Joins-dataonly.qvf

//2 tables for join examples

Users:

LOAD * INLINE [

Name, Department

User1,Dept1

User2,Dept2

User3,Dept3

];

Managers:

LOAD * INLINE [

Department, Manager

Dept1, Manager1

Dept2, Manager2

Dept4, Manager4

];

The key that links the two tables is 'Department' and there are departments that are in both tables as well as a department that is only in the Users\Managers table.

INNER JOIN

INNER JOIN will only display records where there is a matching record in each table.

In this example we will join the Users table with the Managers table, the finished table called 'inner_join_table' will contain all the fields in the Users table and the Department field from the Managers table where the Department field matches.

Add the following code to your loadscript in a new section called 'inner join':

(Advanced\Managing the Qlik Sense Data Model\inner join.txt):

inner_join_table:

//The Noconcatenate option is to prevent the table being concatenated with the inline table.

NoConcatenate

LOAD

Name

,Department

Resident Users;

// Inner join - If no table name is specified then the previously created table is used for the join.

// In this case the join statement: inner join (inner_join_table)

// would have given the same result.

inner join

LOAD

Manager

,Department

Resident Managers;

//We drop the original inline tables so that we don't create synthetic keys.

drop tables Users,Managers;

NOTE: Make sure the new section is below the 'join data' section otherwise you will get an error.

When you reload the loadscript, go to the DMV you can preview the data which should be the same as the screenshot below:

Preview of data

Name	Department	Manager
User1	Dept1	Manager1
User2	Dept2	Manager2

Completed App:

Advanced\Managing the Qlik Sense Data Model\Joins-after Inner join.qvf

Outer Join

An outer join allows rows that do not match to still be included in the final table.

The 'outer join' will combine all rows from both tables whether they are matching or not.

1. Comment out the previous join example.

2. Create a section called 'outer join' and add the following:

outer_join_table:

NoConcatenate

LOAD

Name

,Department

Resident Users;

outer join (outer_join_table)

LOAD

Manager

,Department

Resident Managers;

drop tables Users,Managers;

3. When you reload the app and look at the DMV you should see a single table.

If you preview the table by selecting the table and clicking the preview bar at the bottom of the screen you will see the following data that shows the combination of all rows from both User and Manager tables as shown:(Notice the Null values displayed as '-')

Preview of data

Name	Department	Manager
User1	Dept1	Manager1
User2	Dept2	Manager2
User3	Dept3	-
-	Dept4	Manager4

Completed App:

Advanced\Managing the Qlik Sense Data Model\Joins-after Outer join.qvf

LEFT JOIN

When joining tables together the first table that is part of the join is also known as the left table, whereas the second table used is known as the right table. In this example:

LEFT TABLE = Users table

RIGHT TABLE = Managers table

If you change the following line in the previous example:

outer join (outer_join_table)

to

left join (outer_join_table)

In this example all the rows in the first table which is the Users table have been included and only matching rows in the second (Managers) table.

RIGHT JOIN

A right outer join is simply the opposite of a left outer join, where all the rows of the right table are listed.

Change the left outer join to a right outer join by making the following change:

left join (outer_join_table)

to

right join (outer_join_table)

Reload the app and you will see that the Managers table which is the right table in this example is the one that has all the rows listed.

KEEP

The Keep option is similar to JOIN but does not merge the tables.

The rows are removed in the same way as a join but the tables remain separate.

This is a useful option when you just want to reduce the data in the tables but not actually change the structure of your data model.

Inner Keep Example

1. Go to the DLE in the Joins apps.

2. Comment out previous join examples.

3. Create a new section called 'keep' and add the following:

Users_table:

NoConcatenate

LOAD Name,Department Resident Users;

Managers_table:

inner keep LOAD Manager,Department Resident Managers;

drop tables Users,Managers;

4. When you reload the app and view the tables if will appear as if nothing has changed.

If you preview the data in the tables you will see that only matching rows remain in the tables as shown in the screenshots of each table below:

Managers_table:

Preview of data

Department	Manager
Dept1	Manager1
Dept2	Manager2

Users_table:

Preview of data

Department	Name
Dept1	User1
Dept2	User2

Completed App:

Advanced\Managing the Qlik Sense Data Model\Joins-after Keep.qvf

SUMMARY

Using joins you can create a cleaner data model which in turn will make the creation of your user interface easier to develop and maintain.

CALENDAR TABLES

Often when analyzing data you want to have a table of dates that you can use to link to the data you are importing.

Starting App:

Advanced\Calendar Tables\Order Details-before calendar.qvf

1. Open the Order Details app and go to the DLE. Create a new section called 'Calendar'.

To generate such as table you can add the following script to your load script:

Calendar:

LOAD *

,Month(OrderDate) as OrderMonth

,year(OrderDate) as OrderYear;

LOAD date(makedate(1998)+recno()-1) as OrderDate

AUTOGENERATE 365;

2. The makedate() function returns the date calculated from the Year, Month and Date in the following format:

Makedate(YYYY,MM,DD)

The only parameter that is required in the makedate() function is YYYY.

If MM is omitted then it uses the 1st January.

If DD is omitted then the 1st of the month is used.

3. In our expression for the Date field we only use the year (in this case 1998) so the dates start from the 1st January 1998.

4. We then add 1 substracted from the current row number to the date.

5. Therefore the first date will be 1st January because the row number function recno() starts from 1 so you will be adding nothing to the function makedate(1998).

LOAD date(makedate(1998)+recno()-1)

6. As the row number generated by recno() increases so will be date generated by the date() function.

7. The AUTOGENERATE command repeats the command. In this case it will generate dates for the whole of the year 1998.

If you go to the DMV you will see that the Calendar table has been created and linked to the Orders table because the Date field is set to OrderDate.

8. Drag a filter pane to the sheet and add the dimension OrderYear and OrderMonth. Now you can easily select the year\month you wish to display order details for.

Completed App:

Advanced\Calendar Tables\Order Details-after-calendar 1998.qvf

Calendar using all dates

In the previous calendar example we just generated the dates for 1 year.Next we will extend the idea of creating a calendar table and use all the possible orderdates that exist.

The script used in this example is available in the file:

Advanced\Calendar Tables\calendar - all orderdates.txt.

1. Open the 'Order Details' app and go to the DLE.

2. In the Calendar section (create one if it doesn't already exist) add the following script replace the Calendar table if one already exists:

To create this next Calendar table we first find the earliest and latest date:

OrdersTemp:

LOAD

min(OrderDate) AS minDate,

max(OrderDate) AS maxDate

RESIDENT

orders;

LET   MinOrderDate   =   Num(Peek('minDate',   0, 'OrdersTemp'));

LET   MaxOrderDate   =   Num(Peek('maxDate',   0, 'OrdersTemp'));

DROP TABLE OrdersTemp;

This code finds the min\max date and then uses the Peek function to save each of the minDate\maxDate fields to a variable.

3. Next we create a temp calendar consisting of a date field and the numeric value of the date field.

//Temp Calendar

temp_DateField:

LOAD

$(MinOrderDate) + rowno() -1 as Num,

date($(MinOrderDate) + rowno() -1) as TempDate

AUTOGENERATE$(MaxOrderDate)-$(MinOrderDate)+1;

As an example if the numeric of the min and max dates were 4000 and 4007 then the AUTOGENERATE would actually be

AUTOGENERATE 4007 - 4000+1;

Which would generate 8 rows with values from 1-8:

AUTOGENERATE 8

The date field is then generated using the MinOrderDate value (4000) and the rowno()-1 so this would use the following values converted to a date:

4000, 4001 ... 4007

4. Next we create an orderdate table using the dates we generated:

//OrderDate Calendar

orderdate_calendar:

LOAD

TempDate as [Current Order Date],

Week(TempDate) AS OrderWeek,

Year(TempDate) as OrderYear,

Month(TempDate) as OrderMonth,

Day(TempDate) as OrderDay

Resident temp_DateField

ORDER BY TempDate ASC;

DROP TABLE temp_DateField;

5. Before you reload the loadscript by clicking the 'Load data' button make sure the Calendar section is the last section otherwise you will get errors because it cannot use the orders table.

6. Go to the 'Order Details' sheet, if you followed the previous calendar example you will see that the OrderMonth\OrderYear fields have been updated to include all possible OrderDate years. If the OrderMonth\ OrderYear filters don't exist on your see drag a filter pane to the see and add the dimensions OrderYear and OrderMonth.

7. Click done and save. The OrderMonth and OrderYear filters should look like the following screenshot:

Q OrderYear	Q OrderMonth
1996	Jan
1997	Feb
1998	Mar
	Apr
	May
	Jun
	Jul
	Aug
	Sep
	Oct
	Nov

Now you can use these filters to make selections.

8. Add the dimension 'Current Order Date' to the filter pane so you can check that the filters are working correctly and including the correct dates for each month\year when selected:

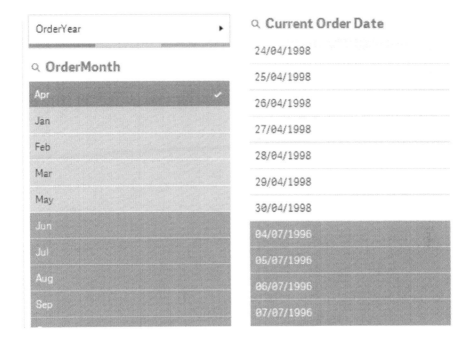

Completed App:

Advanced\Calendar Tables\Order Details-after-calendar-alldates.qvf

ADVANCED FUNCTIONS

OVERVIEW

In this chapter we are going to cover various techniques used when scripting in Qlik Sense and also some of the more advanced functions.

Below are listed the techniques and functions that will be covered in this chapter:

- Preceding Loads
- File Functions
- Class
- Aggr
- IntervalMatch
- Date Functions
- Variables
- Alt

As you progress with your Qlik Sense development you will begin to use these functions more and more.

Here we will cover an introduction to these functions so you are aware of some of the functions available to you.

SAMPLE DATA SETUP

1. Create a new app called 'Advanced Functions'.

2. Create a new sheet called functions.

3. Drag and drop the spreadsheet 'SampleOrderReports. xls' to the sheet.

4. Load the SourceData$ sheet as shown:

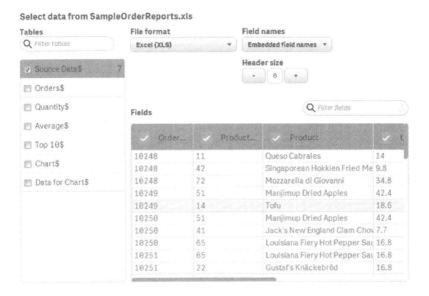

5. Click Edit sheet, then Click Save.

6. Go to the DLE.

7. In the SampleOrderReports.xls section add a table name of 'Orders' to your sample code and reload the data.

Orders:

LOAD

"Order ID",

"Product ID",

Product,

"Unit Price",

Quantity,

Discount,

"Extended Price"

FROM 'lib://data sources/SampleOrderReports.xls'

(biff, embedded labels, table is [Source Data$]);

Now you are ready to start the advanced function examples.

PRECEDING LOADS

Using this technique you can add multiple load statements to perform multiple transformations to the table of data in one go.

This is a similar way in which you perform a SELECT followed by a LOAD statement based on the results returned from the SELECT statement. In this case we are performing a LOAD statement based on the results returned from another LOAD statement.

In the example below the Total Price field is calculated based on the data returned from the load statement below it.

Because you can have multiple preceding loads you can build up quite complex expressions if required.

1. Open the 'advanced functions' app and go to the DLE.

2. Select the SampleOrderReports.xls section in the left pane.

3. Add another load statement to the Orders table under the table name.

LOAD

*,

"Unit Price" * Quantity as "Total Price"

;

The * loads all the fields from the first LOAD statement. Instead of using '*' you could list the fieldnames that were used in the first LOAD statement which you would need to do if you wanted to replace the value and keep the same field name.

4. The full example should look like this:

Orders:

LOAD

*,

"Unit Price" * Quantity as "Total Price"

;

LOAD

"Order ID",

"Product ID",

Product,

"Unit Price",

Quantity,

Discount,

"Extended Price"

FROM 'lib://data sources/SampleOrderReports.xls'

(biff, embedded labels, table is [Source Data$]);

5. Go to the DMV and check that the 'Total Price' field has been created.

The 'Total Price' field is the total value without the discount whereas the 'Extended Price' field contains the value of the order with the discount.

FILE FUNCTIONS

Starting App:

Advanced\Advanced   Functions\File   Functions\ Advanced Functions-before execute.qvf.

Filelist

Filelist function is used to get a list of files in a directory.

In the example below you pass the path to the folder to the filelist directory and use a 'FOR EACH' loop to count the number of files in a folder.

SET vcount = 0;

FOR EACH vFileName IN FILELIST ('C:\somefolder*. txt');

LET vcount = vcount + 1;

NEXT vFileName;

Filelist Example

1. Create the folder c:\filefolder.

2. Within c:\ filefolder create some text files.

3. Open the 'Advanced functions' app and go to the DLE.

4. Create a section called 'file functions'.

Add the following code:

SET vcount = 0;

FOR EACH vFileName IN FILELIST ('C:\filefolder*.txt');

LET vcount = vcount + 1;

NEXT vFileName;

5. Click load data.

6. Create a new sheet.

7. Drag and drop a 'Text & Image' object onto the sheet.

8. Set the expression to the following to count of files in your folder:

='File count = ' &vcount

The function dirlist is similar to filelist but instead of files dirlist will return the names of folders that exist, for example:

for each dir in dirlist('C:\filefolder*')

...Do something

next dir

Completed App: Advanced\Advanced Functions\File Functions\Advanced Functions-after filelist.qvf

Execute

The Execute command can be very useful for executing command line statements during the loadscript. For example creating folders to store qvds, copying files or running other programs.

2 examples below copy a field and create a folder where the name of the folder is in a variable:

Execute cmd.exe /C copy /Y "..\test_folder\myfile.txt" "..\target_folder \";

Execute cmd.exe /C mkdir "..\somefolder\"$(foldername_variable);

Execute Example

1. Create the folders:

C:\filefolder\source

C:\filefolder\destination

2. Create an text file in the folder C:\filefolder\source.

3. Within the 'Advanced functions' app go to the DLE.

4. In the 'file functions' section add the following code:

//Move each file in the source folder to the destination folder

FOR EACH vFileName IN FILELIST('C:\filefolder\source*.txt');

LET currFile = SubField('$(vFileName)','\',-1);

Execute c:\windows\system32\cmd.exe /C move /Y "C:\filefolder\source\$(currFile)" "C:\filefolder\destination\$(currFile)";

NEXT vFileName;

This code will loop around the text files in 'C:\filefolder\source\' folder.

The subfield splits the string using the '\' delimiter and

then returns the last string which should be the filename.

Then the Execute statement runs the move command using cmd.exe.

The execute statement is useful for moving files and creating folders.

Completed App:

Advanced\Advanced Functions\File Functions\ Advanced Functions-after execute.qvf

CLASS

The class function allows you to arrange values into buckets.

This gives you the option to analyse your data using dimensions that did not already exist in the data.

In the next example we will use the class function to count the number of orders that have a discount in groups of 5%.

For example the bar chart will display the number of orders with a discount between 0 and 5%, 5 and 10% as so on.

Class Example

1. Open the 'Advanced functions' app the edit the 'My new sheet' sheet.

2. Go to the DLE.

3. Create a new section called class.

4. Add the following code to the class section.

discount_buckets:

LOAD

"Order ID",

class(Discount*100,5,'value') as Discount%

Resident Orders;

This code uses the class function to group the Discount field values buckets of 5 (second parameter).

Because the Discount field is stored as a percentage we

multiple the number by 100, so for example .1 (which would be 10%) is used in the class function as 10.

The table name is called discount_buckets, we have included the "Order ID" so we have a link to the orders table.

The third parameter of 'value' is text used in the field between the lower and upper values of the bucket.

5. Click load data, then go to the DMV to check the buckets have been created as expected.

Preview of data

10267	15 <= value < 20
10267	0 <= value < 5
10267	15 <= value < 20
10268	0 <= value < 5
10268	0 <= value < 5
10269	5 <= value < 10
10269	5 <= value < 10

You can see from the preview table that the class function has identified which range of values (sometimes called a bucket) each discount value belongs to.

6. Open and edit the sheet already created in this app.

7. In the master items section create a new dimension using the Discount% field.

8. Create a measure called 'Order ID Count' using the expression: count("Order ID").

9. Drag a bar chart to the sheet and add the Dimension 'Discount%' and Measure 'Order ID Count' you have just created.

10. Set the title to 'Orders Discounted Greater than 5%' and in the bar chart properties select Data->Add data->Dimension-> select the 'Discount%' dimension,

set the limitation to Fixed number,

select Bottom, and finally

set the expression to:

count(distinct Discount%)-1

This expression will count the number of discount% buckets and substract 1, this will have the affect of not showing the first bucket in the chart.

Finally take the tick out of the 'Show others' option.

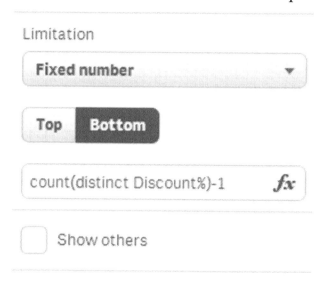

11. In the properties pane set Value Labels to Auto in Appearance-Presentation.

Click the done, then the save button. Your chart should look like the following screenshot:

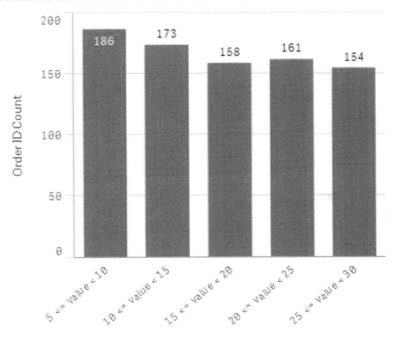

Completed App:

Advanced Functions\Class\Advanced Functions-after class.qvf

AGGR - ADVANCED AGGREGATION

The aggr function allows you to calculate expressions over dimensions.

FORMAT:

aggr([distinct\nodistinct]expression,dimensions)

For example, To sum the total sales amount by country:

aggr(Sum(Sales),Country)

If you add the keyword nodistinct then each combination of dimensions can have 1+ values.

AGGR(nodistinct Sum(Sales),Country)

In this example we will create a bar chart and table to display the maximum quantity sold for each product.

Starting App:

Advanced\Advanced Functions\Aggr - Advanced Aggregation\Advanced Functions-before aggr.qvf

Aggr Example

1. Open the Advanced Functions app.

2. Edit the 'my new sheet' and change the title of the sheet to Orders.

3. Go to the measure items and create a new measure called 'Max Quantity by Product' with an expression of:

Aggr(max(Quantity),Product)

Expression:

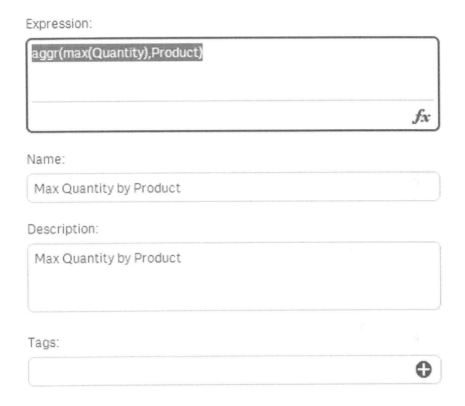

Name:

Max Quantity by Product

Description:

Max Quantity by Product

Tags:

One way to visualize aggr functions is as another table where in this example the Product is a dimension and the max(Quantity) is the measure. So this function will return the maximum Quantity for each Product.

4. Create another measure in the master items Sum(Quantity) called Quantity. You can do this by either just creating a new measure in the master items with an expression of Quantity or going to the fields tab in the left pane, right click on the Quantity field -> Create measure.

5. Add the dimension Product to the master items and drag a table object to the sheet, add the dimension Order ID.

6. Add to the table the Dimension 'Order ID'.

7. Add the following measures to the table:

Quantity

Max Quantity by Product

8. Drag a bar chart to the sheet and add the Dimension Product and a measure of Max Quantity by Product.

9. Set the Label Values to Auto in the Appearance->Presentation section of the properties pane.

10. Click the Save and done button. You can use the bar chart to select a Product.

11. Edit the sheet and select the table you have just created.

12. Go to the sorting section in the properties for the table and drag the Quantity column to the No. 1 position as shown:

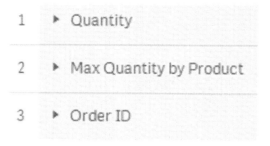

13. Notice that most of the values in the 'Max Quantity by Product' column in the table have dashes instead of values.

Next we will alter the expression so that if there is no value returned a 0 will be displayed.

14. Go back to the master items and edit the measure 'Max Quantity by Product'

15. Change the expression to by surrounding the aggr function with the alt function:

alt(aggr(max(Quantity),Product),0)

The alt expression simple returns the second parameter (0 in this case) if a valid number is not returned by the first parameter (the aggr function).

16. Click Save and Done to view the objects.

I have selected the product: Chartreuse verte

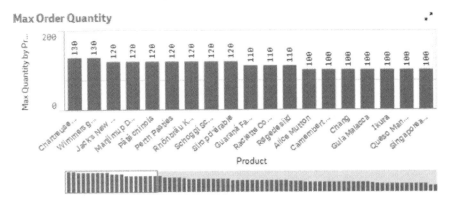

Order Quantity

Order ID	Quantity	Max Quantity by Product
Totals	~	130
10764	130	0
10865	80	0
10297	60	0
10361	54	0
10347	50	0
10895	45	0
10253	42	130

Max Order Quantity

Completed App:

Advanced\Advanced Functions\Aggr - Advanced Aggregation\Advanced Functions-aggr-after.qvf

INTERVAL MATCH

The IntervalMatch function can be used to map dates to periods \ slowly changing dimensions.

An example of a slowly changing dimension might be a user moving between different departments, where if you wanted to display the number of users within a department accurately by month you might take into the account the date they started\ended in the department.

Interval match has the same functionality as BETWEEN in SQL.

IntervalMatch() creates synthetic tables therefore there can be a high RAM\UI performance cost to using this function. One solution to this is to LEFT JOIN the interval match into a parent table to create a cleaner data model.

Next we will demonstrate how to use the interval match function using a simple example.

Starting App:

Advanced\Advanced Functions\Interval Match\ Advanced Functions-intervalmatch-before.qvf

Interval Match Example

1. Open the 'Advanced Functions' sheet and create a sheet called 'Other Functions'. In the 'Other Functions' sheet we will place examples of various advanced functions.

2. Go to the DLE.

3. Create a new section called 'interval match'

4. Add the following script to the 'interval match' section. You can copy the script from the file:

Advanced\ Advanced Functions\ Interval Match\

intervalmatch example.txt

IntervalMatch_TabA:

LOAD * INLINE [

Time

1

2

3

4

5

6

7

8

9

10

];

IntervalMatch_TabB:

LOAD * INLINE [

Emp, Start, Stop

1, 2, 6

2, 3, 7

3, 1, 4

4, 2, 10

];

INNER JOIN(IntervalMatch_TabB)

INTERVALMATCH(Time)

LOAD DISTINCT

Start,

Stop

RESIDENT IntervalMatch_TabB;

5. The function used is IntervalMatch(Time) where the Time field is used to match between the start and stop interval.

6. Reload the document and go to the DMV. You will see that the 2 tables IntervalMatch_TabA and IntervalMatch_TabB have been created.

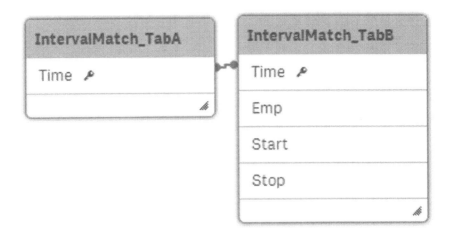

7. The inner join to IntervalMatch_TabB is required to prevent synthetic tables. If you remove the inner join and reload the document you will get the following table structure:

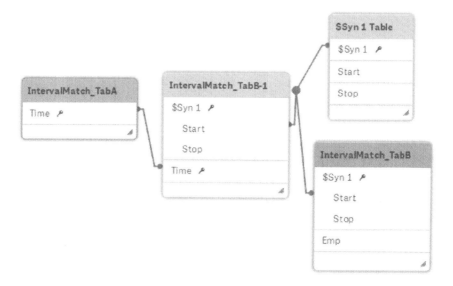

8. Add the inner join back if you removed it and reload the document again.

9. IntervalMatch_TabA contains the inline table with the time values ranging from 1-10.

10. Preview IntervalMatch_TabB should display the following data:

Preview of data

Time	Emp	Start	Stop
2	1	2	6
3	1	2	6
4	1	2	6
5	1	2	6
6	1	2	6
2	4	2	10

11. You can see from this data Emp 1 has a Start value of 2 and Stop value of 6 the Time field goes from 2-6.

DATE FUNCTIONS

There are 2 Date() functions used in qlik sense , Date() and Date#():

Date(expression,[format code])

Date() can be used for formatting the date and returning a string.

Date() evaluates the expression as a date string according to the format code if supplied, for example:

=Date(Floor(LocalTime()),'YY-MM-DD')

Might return: 13-06-21

Date#(expression,[format code])

Date#() is called an interpretation function and evaluates the expression as a number.

Both these functions return a type of Dual which means the users can see the date in the correct string format but the numeric version of the date can be used for sorting and comparisions.

NOTE: If there is no format code the function uses the operating system date format normally set at the start of the loadscript ie: SET *DateFormat*='DD/MM/YYYY';

Setup for examples

1. To test these examples in qlik sense. Open the 'Advanced Functions' go to the 'Other function sheet and edit it.

2. The drag and drop a 'Text & Image' object to the sheet.

3. Select the 'Text & Image' object.

4. In the properties for the 'Text & Image' object select 'Add measure', here you can add an expression that will be added to the text object.

DATE AND TIME

If the date field includes the time it will not be a whole number

For example:

1. Create a text object and create a measure:

=num(today())

2. This will display the current date as a number such as 41431.

Whereas if you change the formula to use LocalTime() so that the date and time is displayed:

=num(LocalTime())

3. You will get a number such as 41431.806331019.

4. Remove the num() function to use just LocalTime() and the string will be converted back to the current date\ time:

08/10/2014 19:21:25

5. If you wanted to remove the time from the LocalTime() function you could use the Floor() function which has the effect of rounding down the numeric value of the date\ time, then apply the date() function to display the date as a string.

=Date(Floor(LocalTime()))

REMEMBER: Because the date is stored as a string\ numeric if you are using timestamp fields you will need to use the formula date(floor(timestampfield)) to remove the time from the field if you need to compare only by dates.

VARIABLES

Starting App:

Advanced\Advanced Functions\Variables\Advanced Functions-before-variables.qvf.

LET OR SET

The default is LET if you leave out the SET\LET statement.

For example add the following line to your loadscript and reload it:

my_test_var = today();

my_test_var has been set to today's date.

SET

Set does not evaluated the expression after the '='.

At the start of the loadscript we set various variables to strings using the SET:

SET *TimeFormat*='hh:mm:ss';

LET

Let evaluates the expression before setting the variable.

For example: To evaluated a function and retrieve a date we use the Let statement.

LET *incremental_load_lastdate* = timestamp(Peek('incremental_load_table.created_dttm',-1),'DD/MM/YYYY HH:MM:SS');

Using variables - Dollar Sign Expansion

To use the variable you have created you can enclose the variable name in the following format:

$(variablename)

For example, add the following code to your loadscript in the DLE and reload the script:

my_test_var = today();

trace $(my_test_var);

This will output today's date.

USING PARAMETERS WITH VARIABLES

You can add parameters to your variables, for example to call my_test_var with 1 parameter:

my_test_var(1)

When you are creating the variable to replace any parameter with $1, $2 and so on. $0 contains the number of parameters.

In this example the variable will contain the following

addmonths function:

'Addmonths(today(),$1)';

The addmonths function adds a number of months to the date in the first parameter of the addmonths function using the 2nd parameter.

In this example the 2nd parameter of the add months function is set to $1 which will be the first (and only) parameter we pass to the variable.

Add the following script to your loadscript and reload:

my_test_var = 'addmonths(today(),$1)';

LET result = $(my_test_var(1));

trace $(result);

Reload the app, the result that is returned will be the current date + 1 month.

To use multiple parameters just separate them with commas

For example:

my_test_var = 'addmonths(today(),$1+$2)';

LET result = $(my_test_var(1,2));

NO DOLLAR SIGN EXPANSION REQUIRED

If you are using simple text in your variable you do not require a Dollar sign expansion.

For example:

1. Create the variable in the DLE using SET:

SET myvar = 'no DSE required';

2. Then within a 'text and image' object add the measure:

=myvar

This would display the text in the myvar variable

SQL STORED PROCEDURES

Update a SQL server table from the loadscript

It is possible to update SQL server tables using a stored procedure call when reloading your Qlik Sense app.

The code to create the table and stored procedure can be found in the file: Advanced\Advanced Functions\SQL stored procedures\create users table and procedure.txt

1. Run the follow code to create a users table.

CREATE TABLE [dbo].[users](

[id] [int] IDENTITY(1,1) NOT NULL,

[name] [nchar](50) NULL,

[created_dttm] [date] NULL

)

2. Add a stored procedure to the SQL server:

CREATE PROCEDURE update_from_qv

@username varchar(100)

AS

BEGIN

INSERT INTO dbo.users(name,created_dttm) VALUES(@username,'12/12/14')

select * from users

END

3. Open the 'Advanced Functions' app and in the DLE create a section called SQL.

4. Create a new OLE DB connection to your SQL server and select the database where your stored procedure 'update_from_qv' exists.

5. Click the insert connection string button

LIB CONNECT TO 'SQL server name';

SQL EXECUTE testdb.dbo.update_from_qv @ username='me'

In this example we are passing the variable @username to the stored procedure.

This will add a row to the table users in the database.

Completed App:

Advanced\ Advanced Functions\ SQL stored procedures\ Advanced Functions-after SQL.qvf

DUAL FUNCTION

The dual command associates a number with a string.

The main reason you might want to do this is to sort string field numerically rather than alphabetically.

For example, imagine that you had and OrderID and Status field where the OrderID was a number and the Status could be any of the following:

- started

- processing

- completed

Starting App:

Advanced\Advanced   Functions\Dual   Function\ Advanced Functions-before dual.qvf

For example:

1. Go to the 'Advanced Functions' app and in the DLE create the section dual.

2. Add the following table:

(See file Advanced\Advanced Functions\Dual Function\ dual table.txt)

dualdata:

LOAD * Inline

[dual_orderid, dual_status

1, started

2, completed

3, processing

4, completed

5, started

];

This table contains and orderid value and a status.

2. Edit the sheet 'Other functions' and create a table.

3. Add the fields dual_orderid and dual_status to the table as dimensions:

4. Click Done and Save and your table should look the following:

dual_orderid Q	dual_status
1	started
2	completed
3	processing
4	completed
5	started

5. Edit the sheet again and select the table, give the table a title such as 'Dual Table'.

6. Select the table and in the properties pane, sorting drag dual_status to be first as shown:

Sorting	
1	▸ dual_status
2	▸ dual_orderid

7. You can see that the status is being sorted alphabetically:

Dual Table

dual_orderid Q	dual_status
2	completed
4	completed
3	processing
1	started
5	started

Ideally we would like the status to be sorted in the order: Started, Processing, Completed.

We can do this using the dual function.

Go to the dual section in the DLE, you can either make the changes manually of replace the code with the script you will find in the file:

Advanced\Advanced Functions\Dual Function\dual solution.txt.

The changes that need to be make are:

1. rename the table of data from dualdata to dualdata_ temp.

2. Add the mapping load that will be used in the dual function to return a numeric value associated with the string.

//Create a mapping between the status and a number

status_to_num:

MAPPING LOAD * INLINE

[

started,1

processing,2

completed,3

];

3. Create another table called dualdata. The dualdata table will use the data in the dualdata_temp table using the resident keyword.

The NoConcatenate keyword before the LOAD prevents the data in the dualdata and dualdata_temp tables being automatically concatenated just because they have the same field names in both tables.

Next in the LOAD statement we include the field dual_ orderid, then the dual_status field created using the dual function.

dualdata:

NoConcatenate LOAD

dual_orderid,

dual(dual_status,

ApplyMap('status_to_num',dual_status,0)

) as dual_status

Resident dualdata_temp;

The first parameter = the string representation of the field - in this case the dual_status field.

The second parameter = the numeric representation of the field.

In this example we using the applymap function to return the numeric value and 0 if none exists in the mapping load table 'status_to_num'.

ApplyMap('status_to_num',dual_status,0)

4. Click the load data button and go back to the 'Other functions' sheet and the 'Dual table' you created.

Your table should now be sorted in the order:

Started,Processing,Completed as shown:

Dual Table

dual_orderid	dual_status
1	started
5	started
3	processing
2	completed
4	completed

Completed App:

Advanced\Advanced Functions\Dual Function\ Advanced Functions-after dual.qvf

SET ANALYSIS

Set-analysis is used with aggregation functions ie: functions do something to a set of fields.

For example a function might add up the total of a set of numbers, this would be the sum() function.

Currently Qlik Sense has been using the current selection to decide what is included in this set of numbers when you use the sum() function but you can change the set using set analysis.

A set is defined in curly brackets {}

$ = the current selection in this example this could be one month.

So the sum(Spent) expression = Sum({$} Spent)

Another simple example would be the following expression which will sum the total of the spent field has a category of food:

Sum({ $<Category={Food}> } Spent)

AGGREGATION FUNCTIONS

When starting to use aggregation functions and set analysis it is useful to create a file with the initial structure of set analysis command. For example:

Sum({ $<Dim1={Value1}> } Field)

You can easily see that using an expression template such as this would save time and reduce mistakes when creating what context expressions, especially those set analysis.

Sample data

1. Create a new app called 'Order Details' and open the app.

2. Drag and drop the spreadsheet SampleOrderData.xls to the app and import the Orders sheet as shown:

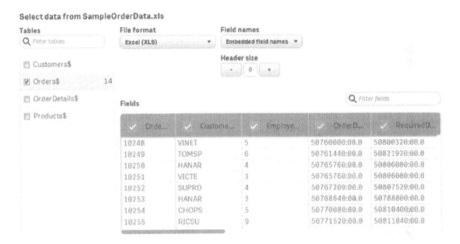

3. Replace the SampleOrderData.xls LOAD statement with the following script:

This will load the order and order details:

(see file Advanced\Set Analysis\set analysis sample load. txt)

orders:

LOAD OrderID,

CustomerID,

EmployeeID,

date(OrderDate) as OrderDate,

```
date(RequiredDate) as RequiredDate,

date(ShippedDate) as ShippedDate,

ShipVia,

Freight,

ShipName,

ShipAddress,

ShipCity,

ShipRegion,

ShipPostalCode,

ShipCountry

FROM 'lib://data sources/SampleOrderData.xls'

(biff, embedded labels, table is Orders$);

order_details:

LOAD

OrderID,

ProductID,

UnitPrice,

Quantity,

Discount

FROM 'lib://data sources/SampleOrderData.xls'

(biff, embedded labels, table is OrderDetails$);
```

4. Click the load button again, save the app.

5. Go to the DMV to check the data from the Orders and OrderDetails sheets in the spreadsheet have been loaded into your app.

Completed App:

Advanced\Set Analysis\Order Details-after sampledata. qvf

WILDCARDS

1. Create a new sheet in the 'Order Details' apps called 'Order Details'.

2. Create a new table.

You can use wildcards such as '*' to replace 1 or more characters.

In this example we will use the following set analysis expression to calculate the sum of Quantity*UnitPrice for all CustomerID's that start with AN:

=sum({$<CustomerID={"AN*"}>}Quantity*UnitPrice)

Dimension 1 – List of customer ids.

Measure 1 – The sum of Quantity * UnitPrice for the current selection, using the expression:

=sum(Quantity*UnitPrice)

Set the Number formatting of this column to Money.

Set the Label to 'Total Price'.

Measure 2 - The sum of Quantity * UnitPrice for the current selection for all records in the document but for only the cutomer ids that are with 'AN':

=sum({1<CustomerID={"AN*"}>}Quantity*UnitPrice)

Set the Number formatting of this column to Money.

Set the Label to 'AN Customers Total Price'.

The screenshot shows a table shows 3 columns described:

Order Details

CustomerID	Total Price	AN Customers Total Price
Totals	£1,354,458.59	£8,918.30
ALFKI	£4,596.20	£0.00
ANATR	£1,402.95	£1,402.95
ANTON	£7,515.35	£7,515.35
AROUT	£13,806.50	£0.00
BERGS	£26,968.15	£0.00
BLAUS	£3,239.80	£0.00
BLONP	£19,088.00	£0.00
BOLID	£5,297.80	£0.00
BONAP	£23,850.95	£0.00
BOTTM	£22,607.70	£0.00
BSBEV	£6,089.90	£0.00
CACTU	£1,814.80	£0.00
CENTC	£100.80	£0.00
CHOPS	£12,886.30	£0.00
COMMI	£3,810.75	£0.00
CONSH	£1,719.10	£0.00
DRACD	£3,763.21	£0.00
DUMON	£1,615.90	£0.00

The customerID 'ANTON' has been selected, but because of the set analysis in column 3 the customer starting ANATR and ANTON are also included in the table.

Order Details

CustomerID Q	Total Price	AN Customers Total Price
Totals	£7,515.35	£8,918.30
ANATR	£0.00	£1,402.95
ANTON	£7,515.35	£7,515.35

The expression used in column 2 which is =sum(Quantity*UnitPrice) does not include any set analysis and therefore defaults to using the current selection.

Because we are using '1' instead of '$' (the current selection) in our set analysis the expression is not limited to the current selection.

Completed App:

Advanced\Set Analysis\Order Details-after wildcard.qvf

DATE FIELD EXAMPLE

In this example we will show how you can use date fields with set analysis.

1. Open the 'Order Details' app. Open the 'Order Details' sheet and click the edit button.

2. Drag a table object to the sheet.

3. Add the Dimension CustomerID.

4. Then click 'add column' to add the following expression as a measure:

=count(distinct OrderID)

Set the label of this measure to 'Order Count'.

Your table should look like the following screenshot:

CustomerID	Q	Order Count
Totals		830
ALFKI		6
ANATR		4
ANTON		7
AROUT		13
BERGS		18
BLAUS		7
BLONP		11
BOLID		3

5. Next we will add another measure column to the table. Call the column Orders from 1998.

The new column would calculate the number of orders for each customer after a certain date.

The set analysis we will use to make this calculation is displayed below:

=Count({1 <OrderDate={">=$(=Date('1/1/1998', 'DD/ MM/YYYY'))"}>} DISTINCT OrderID)

CustomerID Q	Order Count	Orders from 1998
Totals	830	270
ALFKI	6	3
ANATR	4	1
ANTON	7	1
AROUT	13	4
BERGS	18	5
BLAUS	7	3
BLONP	11	1
BOLID	3	1

This set analysis uses a 1 after the first { to indicate that the current selection will be ignored and counts the distinct OrderID's where the OrderDate is greater than the following expression:

=$(=Date('1/1/1998', 'DD/MM/YYYY'))

Which is simply the date function surrounded by a dollar expansion $() which simple converts the function into text to use in the set analysis.

6. If you would like to use set analysis to display a count of orders between two dates you can use the asterix symbol(*) as shown in the next example.

7. In this example we will add an extra measure column that will display a count of the orders between 1/1/98 and 3/3/98 this,call this column 'Orders between dates':

=Count({1 <OrderDate= {">=$(=Date('1/1/1998', 'DD/MM/YYYY'))"} * {"<=$(=Date('3/3/1998', 'DD/MM/YYYY'))"} >} DISTINCT OrderID)

Your table should now look like the following screenshot:

CustomerID	Q	Order Count	Orders from 1998	Orders between dates
Totals		830	270	116
ALFKI		6	3	1
ANATR		4	1	0
ANTON		7	1	1
AROUT		13	4	2
BERGS		18	5	4
BLAUS		7	3	1
BLONP		11	1	1

8. The asterix symbol (*) is used to return the records that belong to both sets, in set analysis the asterix symbol is called a set modifier.

Other types of set modifiers are:

+ This will return records that belong to the either set.

- This will return records that belong to the first set but not the second set.

/ This will return records that only belong to one of the two sets.

9. In this example the two sets are:

Order dates greater than 1/1/1998:

{">=$(=Date('1/1/1998', 'DD/MM/YYYY'))"}

And

Order dates less than 3/3/1998:

{"<=$(=Date('3/3/1998', 'DD/MM/YYYY'))"}

10. If we take one of the sets and look at it in more detail you will see that in mainly consists of the date function:

=Date('3/3/1998', 'DD/MM/YYYY')

11. Wrapped around the date function is the dollar-sign expansion $().

12. QlikView replaces the function in the dollar sign expansion with the date so the set actually becomes:

{"<='3/3/1998'"}

13. Using the dollar sign expansion in this way would be more useful if the date 3/3/1998 was replaced with a function such as today() or a variable, for example:

{"<=$(Today())"}

14. The dollar sign expansion is also useful if you wish to store the function in a variable for example, you could create a variable that contains the following function text:

=Date('3/3/1998', 'DD/MM/YYYY')

SET ANALYSIS AND VARIABLES

You could replace the function in this set analysis with your variable name.

1. Go to the DLE and create the variable vOrderDateLimit:

SET vOrderDateLimit = '1/1/2000';

2. Click the load button and go back to the sheet 'Order Details'.

3. Add the following measure column with a label of 'Using vOrderDateLimit'.

The expression is using the variable name that I created was called vOrderDateLimit:

=Count({1 <OrderDate= {">=$(=Date('1/1/1998', 'DD/ MM/YYYY'))"} * {"<=$(vOrderDateLimit)"} >} DISTINCT OrderID)

4. It is useful to put set analysis expressions in variables so that if you need to make a change you only need to change the variable rather than every object that uses the expression.

Your table should look like the following screenshot:

CustomerID	Order Count	Orders from 1998	Orders between dates	Using vOrderDateLimit
Totals	830	270	116	270
ALFKI	6	3	1	3
ANATR	4	1	0	1
ANTON	7	1	1	1
AROUT	13	4	2	4
BERGS	18	5	4	5
BLAUS	7	3	1	3
BLONP	11	1	1	1
BOLID	3	1	0	1

Completed App:

Advanced\Set Analysis\Order Details-after sa var.qvf

POSSIBLE AND EXCLUDED VALUES

In this example we will look at using the functions p() and e() in set analysis to return a set of values that are either associated with a particular field or not.

You will see how we can use these functions to build set analysis expressions that will answer more complex queries.

P()

The function p() is used to return the set of possible values associated with another value. The format of the p()

function is:

p({set expression} expression)

In the example below this set analysis uses the p() function to count the number of OrderID values for customers that had bought the product 'Chai':

=Count({1<CustomerID=p({1<ProductName={'Chai'}>} CustomerID)>} DISTINCTOrderID)

1. Open the 'Order Details' app and go to the DLE.

2. Add the following script or drag and drop the SampleOrderData.xls spreadsheet to the app and add the Products sheet (find this script in the Advanced\Set Analysis\products.txt file):

products:

LOAD

ProductID,

ProductName,

SupplierID,

CategoryID,

QuantityPerUnit,

// UnitPrice,

UnitsInStock,

UnitsOnOrder,

ReorderLevel,

Discontinued

FROM 'lib://data sources/SampleOrderData.xls'

(biff, embedded labels, table is Products$);

Make sure to name the table 'products' and reload the data.

I have commented out the UnitPrice field because it already exists in another table. If you did not do this a synthetic key would be created.

3. In the 'Order Details' app edit the 'Order Details' sheet.

4. Add the following measure column to the table you have been creating using set analysis

=Count({1<CustomerID=p({1<ProductName={'Chai'}>} CustomerID)>} DISTINCT OrderID)

Set the label to 'CHAI Customer order count' as shown:

CustomerID	Q	Order Count	Orders from 1998	Orders between dates	Using vOrderDateLimit	CHAI Customer order count
Totals	▾	6	278	116	278	369
ALFKI		6	3	1	3	0
ANATR		0	1	0	1	0
ANTON		0	1	1	1	0
AROUT		0	4	2	4	0
BERGS		0	5	4	5	18
BLAUS		0	3	1	3	0
BLONP		0	1	1	1	11
BOLID		0	1	0	1	0

5. If we extract the p() function. You will see that the whole expression is basically made up of one set analysis expression within another.

P({1<ProductName={'Chai'}>}CustomerID)

To make the development of such complex expressions easier. It is sometimes useful to test the set expression used in the p() function separately before adding the p() function to a larger set analysis expression.

One simple way to do this is to use the concat function and

display the set in a text object as shown below. The seperator of '\n' is used to that each CustomerID is displayed on a new line.

=concat({1<ProductName={'Chai'}>} CustomerID,'\n')

Completed App:

Advanced\Set Analysis\Order Details-after sa possible. qvf

SUMMARY

Set analysis can prove useful to create complex calculations based on various selections in the app.

Ideally your apps will contain set analysis only where required especially in charts where the performance of your app can be greatly improved if you keep the expressions used as simple as you can and if using charts will large amounts of data force users to make selections first.

SELECTION AND COUNT FUNCTIONS

Next we will cover various functions that can be used within the sheet to display information on the current selection and counts of fields selected.

These functions are useful when used in conjunction with set analysis to have a dynamic list of variables included\ excluded from the set of data.

Selection Function - GetFieldSelections

For example, open the following app to use with the examples.

Starting App:

Charts and Tables\Chart Groups\Charts-after-drilldown. qvf

With the GetFieldSelections you can return a list of selections for a particular field and the list can be separated by a character such as a comma.

For example: In the charts app create a text & image object with the following expression as a measure:

GetFieldSelections(Customer)

This would return a comma separated list of selected customers.

Whereas the following expression would return that same list separated by semi-colons:

GetFieldSelections(Customer,';')

GetFieldSelections and Set Analysis

The GetFieldSelections function is useful for using within set analysis.

For example you could add the following expression as a measure to a text & image object:

Sum({1<   Customer-={$(=GetFieldSelections(Customer,',''))} >} [Qtr 1])

This expression would calculate the sum of "Qtr 1" for all customers except those that have been selected.

This is the function used within the set analysis:

$(=GetFieldSelections(Customer,','))

We have modified the set of values to be excluded using '-=' instead of '='.

COUNT FUNCTIONS

GetSelectedCount

The GetSelectedCount function will return the number of values selected, for example:

- GetSelectedCount(Customer)
- GetAlternativeCount
- GetPossibleCount
- GetExcludedCount

These functions return the count of the alternative (light gray), possible (white) and excluded (dark gray) values.

WEB FILES

If you have not used the web files connection in the loadscript before you test it using html tables from the Internet such as:

http://en.wikipedia.org/wiki/List_of_countries_with_McDonald%27s_franchises

1. Create a new app and go to the DLE.

2. Click create new connection and select 'Web file'.

3. Enter the URL and a name for the connection and click Save:

http://en.wikipedia.org/wiki/List_of_countries_with_McDonald%27s_franchises

(If this changes in the future just look for another table on the internet)

Select web file

URL

http://en.wikipedia.org/wiki/List_of_countries_with_McDonald%27s_fr

Name

McDonalds

4. Select the second table which is listed as @2, and set the fields names to 'Embedded field names'.

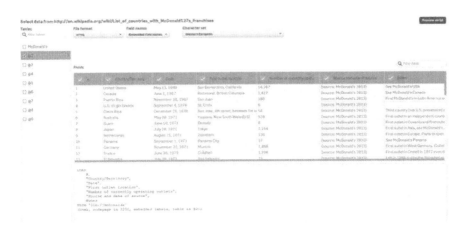

5. Click insert script and add a name to the table, your script should look like the following:

mcdonalds:

LOAD

#,

"Country/Territory",

"Date",

"First outlet location",

"Number of currently operating outlets",

"Source and date of source",

Notes

FROM 'lib://McDonalds'

(html, codepage is 1252, embedded labels, table is @2);

6. Click the reload data button, then go to the DMV to check the data was loaded.

7. You can then create a new sheet with the data in a table and filter panes to being exploring the data.

QVD - QLIK SENSE DATA

WHY USE QVDS?

There are several reasons for using QVDs the main ones being:

1. You will read the data into your app faster (FASTER).

2. You can create incremental loads of data where you only read the records from the data sources that have changed (LESS DATA READ).

3. You can reuse the QVDs in multiple apps (REUSE MEANS EASIER AND FASTER DEVELOPMENT).

Next we will cover several different ways in which you can use QVDs.

USING THE STORE COMMAND

The STORE command can save a full table into a qvd.

Using the format:

STORE <table> INTO <qvd filename including path>.qvd (qvd);

For example:

1. Create a new app called 'first qvd';

2. Go to the DLE , create a section called 'Users QVD' and add the following inline table and the STORE command to create the QVD.

users:

```
LOAD * INLINE [
userid, name
1, Joe
2, Mark
3, Tim
];
```

STORE users INTO C:\users.qvd(qvd);

This command will store the table called users into the c:\ users.qvd file.

If you get the following error, it might mean you don't have permissions to save the qvd to the c:\ drive:

Data load failed

In this case you can :

1. Remove the path in the store command which will create the qvd in the same folder as the app:

STORE users INTO users.qvd(qvd);

Or

2. Create a QVDs folder in the App folder and use a relative path to the QVD folder, for example:

STORE users INTO QVDs\users.qvd(qvd);

Or

3. Add an absolute path to somewhere to do have permissions to save files such as your Document Folder.

You can create a QVDs folder in the documents folder ie:

C:\Users\<username>\Documents\QVDs.

The updated STORE command for me would be the path to your Documents folder will be different:

STORE users INTO C:\Users\techstuffy\Documents\ QVDs

Completed App:

Advanced\QVDs\initial example\first qvd-first example. qvf

TEST THE QVD

1. Create another app called 'read qvd' and in the DLE add the following LOAD statement to use the QVD:

users:

LOAD * from c:\users.qvd(qvd);

2. The output indicates that the qvd was optimized, we will cover later why this is important for performance.

users << user_info

(QVD columnar optimized)

Lines fetched: 3

3. Go to the DMV to check the data was loaded correctly.

Completed App:

Advanced\QVDs\read qvd.qvf

QVD INCREMENTAL LOADING

In this example we will cover an example of how to using incremental loading with QVDs.

Using the incremental loading technique when creating QVD files means that you will have to read only the data that has changed.

If you only need to add\delete rows to the QVD file a Unique field such as an ID field which is an integer is all that is required.

If you need to update rows from the QVD you will require a modification datetime field.

Initial QVD Load

1. Create an app called 'inc qvd'.

2. Go to the DLE and create a new folder to the connection qvd data data sources\qvd , the connection is called 'qvd data'.

3. Create a new section in the DLE called 'User QVD'. Add the following script to the 'Initial QVD' section to create the initial qvd file:

(see file data sources\qvd\initial qvd load.txt)

// Create the inital QVD

IF isNull(QvdCreateTime('c:\users.qvd'))=-1 THEN

TRACE Initial QVD load...;

users:

LOAD id,

username,

[license type],

created,

modified

FROM

'lib://qvd data/inc_qvd.xls'

(biff, embedded labels, table is [Sheet1$]);

IF ScriptErrorCount=0 then

//Save the table into a qvd file

STORE users into c:\users.qvd(qvd);

END IF

END IF

4. This script determines whether or not to create the qvd with an inital load or incremental load using a function called QvdCreateTime that returns the time the qvd was created to check if the qvd file exists.

5. The variable ScriptErrorCount simply counts any error in your script, in this example if there are any script errors we do not create the qvd.

6. Go to the DMV to check that the data was loaded from the spreadsheet inc_qvd.xls:

Preview of data

id	username	license type	created	modified
2	UserB	Named	01/01/2013	07/05/2013
3	UserC	Document	05/04/2013	05/04/2013
4	Mark	Named	06/05/2013	06/05/2013

Completed App:

Advanced\QVDs\inc qvd-initial load.qvf

INCREMENTAL LOAD EXAMPLE

1. Now that we have created the base qvd file with the initial load we will add the code to perform the incremental load.

2. In this example we will explain how we add just the new records added to the Excel spreadsheet.

NOTE: The incremental load is covered in an IF statement so only either the incremental load or base load is run when the app is reloaded.

3. The processes to perform an incremental load just for appended records is simply:

a. Load the current QVD file.

b. Find out the created date of the last record in the Excel spreadsheet.

c. Only read the records from the spreadsheet that have a date greater than the last created date in the QVD.

d. Concatenate the rows read from the current qvd and the new records read from the

spreadsheet.

e. Save the concatenated table into the qvd.

UPDATE THE SAMPLE DATA

To follow this example we are using the spreadsheet data sources\qvd\inc_qvd_append.xls.

Rename the inc_qvd.xls file to inc.qvd.bak and save a copy of inc_qvd_append.xls as inc_qvd.xls.

Alternatively make a copy of the inc.qvd.xls file and update the original file to match the following table.

In this example we have added the extra row to the spreadsheet (username 'Mark'), as shown below:

Id	Username	license type	created	modified
1	UserA	Named	01/04/2012	
2	UserB	Document	01/01/2013	
3	UserC	Document	05/04/2013	
4	Mark	Named	06/05/2013	

See file data sources\qvd\append incremental load.txt for the full script.

```
//Do the incremental load

IF isNull(QvdCreateTime('c:\users.qvd'))=0 THEN

TRACE Incremental load...;

//Load the current qvd file

users:

LOAD * FROM c:\users.qvd(qvd);

//Get the date of the last record created - assuming they
are in date order

LET user_created_maxdate = timestamp(Peek('created',-
1),'DD/MM/YYYY');

DROP TABLE users;

//Load the records that have been added
```

```
noconcatenate users:
LOAD id,
username,
[license type],
created,
modified
FROM 'lib://qvd data/inc_qvd.xls'
(biff, embedded labels, table is [Sheet1$])
where created > '$(user_created_maxdate)';
// Load records that have not been updated from the qvd
UNQUALIFY *;
users:
Concatenate LOAD *
FROM c:\users.qvd(qvd);
IF ScriptErrorCount=0 then
STORE users into c:\users.qvd(qvd);
END IF
END IF
```

5. When you reload the app the following output:

```
users << users
(QVD columnar optimized)
Lines fetched: 3
```

users << Sheet1$

Lines fetched: 4

users << users

Lines fetched: 7

6. From this you can see that:

- 3 lines where read from the current qvd,

- 4 lines fetched - this is the result of concatenating the qvd and new records read from the spreadsheet.

5. Go the the 'read qvd' app created at the start of this chapter and reload the data to check that the qvd has been updated.

Completed App:

Advanced\QVDs\incremental examples\inc qvd-append.qvf

UPDATED ROWS

To change the incremental load script to read rows that have been updated you need to have a modified date field in your spreadsheet.

There are 2 changes required:

1. Start using the modified date field instead of the created date\time field to read new records from the spreadsheet.

2. Add the following command to the final qvd load so that only records not changed are read from the qvd:

WHERE NOT Exists(id name);

So that the final concatenation of the qvd and updated records from the spreadsheet will now be:

users:

Concatenate LOAD *

FROM c:\users.qvd(qvd)

WHERE NOT Exists(id);

NOTE: Remember to move the semi-colon (;) to the end of the WHERE clause.

The full example is:

// Create the inital QVD

IF isNull(QvdCreateTime('c:\users.qvd'))=-1 THEN

TRACE Initial QVD load...;

users:

LOAD id,

username,

[license type],

created,

modified

FROM

'lib://qvd data/inc_qvd.xls'

(biff, embedded labels, table is [Sheet1$]);

IF ScriptErrorCount=0 then

//Save the table into a qvd file

STORE users into c:\users.qvd(qvd);

END IF

//Do the incremental load

ELSEIF isNull(QvdCreateTime('c:\users.qvd'))=0 THEN

TRACE Incremental load...;

//Load the current qvd file

users:

LOAD * FROM c:\users.qvd(qvd);

//Get the date of the last record created - assuming they are in date order

LET user_created_maxdate = timestamp(Peek('created',-1),'DD/MM/YYYY');

DROP TABLE users;

//Load the records that have been added

noconcatenate users:

LOAD id,

username,

[license type],

created,

modified

FROM 'lib://qvd data/inc_qvd.xls'

(biff, embedded labels, table is [Sheet1$])

where created > '$(user_created_maxdate)';

// Load records that have not been updated from the qvd

UNQUALIFY *;

users:

Concatenate LOAD *

FROM c:\users.qvd(qvd)

WHERE NOT Exists(id);

IF ScriptErrorCount=0 then

STORE users into c:\users.qvd(qvd);

END IF

END IF

Completed App:

Advanced\QVDs\inc qvd-update.qvf

UPDATED ROWS EXAMPLE

1. Add modified dates to the spreadheet so they are the same as the created field as shown:

See file data sources\qvd\inc_qvd_add_modified.xls.

id	username	license type	created	modified
1	UserA	Named	01/04/2012	01/04/2012
2	UserB	Document	01/01/2013	01/01/2013
3	UserC	Document	05/04/2013	05/04/2013
4	Mark	Named	06/05/2013	06/05/2013

2. Delete the users.qvd file and reload the app to create the initial qvd.

3. Modify one of the records and update the modified date field. For example see UserB:

See file data sources\qvd\inc_qvd_modified_user.xls.

id	username	license type	created	modified
1	UserA	Named	01/04/2012	01/04/2012
2	UserB	Named	01/01/2013	07/05/2013
3	UserC	Document	05/04/2013	05/04/2013
4	Mark	Named	06/05/2013	06/05/2013

4. Reload the app, you should see the following text in the progress screen if you are using the same data.

Incremental load...

users << users

(QVD columnar optimized)

Lines fetched: 4

users << Sheet1$

Lines fetched: 1

users << users

(QVD columnar optimized)

Lines fetched: 4

Full loadscript used in this example:

See file data sources\qvd\modified incremental load.txt.

// Create the inital QVD

IF isNull(QvdCreateTime('c:\users.qvd'))=-1 THEN

TRACE Initial QVD load...;

```
users:
LOAD id,
username,
[license type],
created,
modified
FROM
'lib://qvd data/inc_qvd.xls'
(biff, embedded labels, table is [Sheet1$]);
IF ScriptErrorCount=0 then
//Save the table into a qvd file
STORE users into c:\users.qvd(qvd);
END IF
//Do the incremental load
ELSEIF isNull(QvdCreateTime('c:\users.qvd'))=0 THEN
TRACE Incremental load...;
//Load the current qvd file
users:
LOAD * FROM c:\users.qvd(qvd);
//Get the date of the last record created - assuming they
are in date order
LET                user_modified_maxdate              =
timestamp(Peek('modified',-1),'DD/MM/YYYY');
```

```
//LETuser_created_maxdate=timestamp(Peek('created',-
1),'DD/MM/YYYY');
DROP TABLE users;
//Load the records that have been added
noconcatenate users:
LOAD id,
username,
[license type],
created,
modified
FROM 'lib://qvd data/inc_qvd.xls'
(biff, embedded labels, table is [Sheet1$])
where modified > '$(user_modified_maxdate)';
//Load records that have not been updated from the qvd
//This can be taken from the QVD or Resident table
UNQUALIFY *;
users:
Concatenate LOAD *
FROM c:\users.qvd(qvd)
WHERE NOT Exists(id);
IF ScriptErrorCount=0 then
STORE users into c:\users.qvd(qvd);
END IF
```

END IF

Completed App:

Advanced\QVDs\inc qvd-modify.qvf

DELETED ROWS EXAMPLE

Finally we will alter the loadscript to update the qvd when rows are deleted from the spreadsheet.

This is simply done by added an inner join command to the spreadsheet so that only rows that match the current spreadsheet are kept in the final table.

INNER JOIN

LOAD id FROM

'lib://qvd data/inc_qvd.xls'

(biff, embedded labels, table is [Sheet1$]);

1. Delete UserA from the spreadsheet inc_qvd.xls as shown:

(see inc_qvd_deleted.xls):

id	username	license type	created	modified
2	UserB	Named	01/01/2013	07/05/2013
3	UserC	Document	05/04/2013	05/04/2013
4	Mark	Named	06/05/2013	06/05/2013

2. Add the inner join statement so your incremental code looks like the code below:

See file data sources\qvd\delete incremental load.txt.

// Create the inital QVD

```
IF isNull(QvdCreateTime('c:\users.qvd'))=-1 THEN

TRACE Initial QVD load...;

users:

LOAD id,

username,

[license type],

created,

modified

FROM

'lib://qvd data/inc_qvd.xls'

(biff, embedded labels, table is [Sheet1$]);

IF ScriptErrorCount=0 then

//Save the table into a qvd file

STORE users into c:\users.qvd(qvd);

END IF

//Do the incremental load

ELSEIF isNull(QvdCreateTime('c:\users.qvd'))=0 THEN

TRACE Incremental load...;

//Load the current qvd file

users:

LOAD * FROM c:\users.qvd(qvd);

//Get the date of the last record created - assuming they
are in date order
```

```
LET user_modified_maxdate =
timestamp(Peek('modified',-1),'DD/MM/YYYY');

//LET user_created_maxdate = timestamp(Peek('created',-
1),'DD/MM/YYYY');

DROP TABLE users;

//Load the records that have been added

noconcatenate users:

LOAD id,

username,

[license type],

created,

modified

FROM 'lib://qvd data/inc_qvd.xls'

(biff, embedded labels, table is [Sheet1$])

where modified > '$(user_modified_maxdate)';

//Load records that have not been updated from the qvd

//This can be taken from the QVD or Resident table

UNQUALIFY *;

users:

Concatenate LOAD *

FROM c:\users.qvd(qvd)

WHERE NOT Exists(id);

INNER JOIN
```

LOAD id FROM

'lib://qvd data/inc_qvd.xls'

(biff, embedded labels, table is [Sheet1$]);

IF ScriptErrorCount=0 then

STORE users into c:\users.qvd(qvd);

END IF

END IF

Reload the app and check the progress shows the same as the text below if you are using the same data. You should note that the last line shows that 1 line less has been read because of the inner join.

Incremental load…

users << users

(QVD columnar optimized)

Lines fetched: 4

users << Sheet1$

Lines fetched: 1

users << users

(QVD columnar optimized)

Lines fetched: 4

users-1 << Sheet1$

Lines fetched: 3

BUFFER STATEMENT

This command uses QVDs to buffer the result of the load statement.

This command can be used to improve performance during reloads by reducing the data that needs to be read from the datasource.

Examples:

Buffer select * from log;

INCREMENTAL - only reads records not read from data sources - updates QVD after.

Buffer (incremental) load * from log;

STALE AFTER - recreates QVD from data source after a time limit:

BUFFER (stale after 7 days) load * from log;

To test this, read in some data from a small text file and add the following buffer command:

NOTE: You will need to use hours even for 1 hour or you will get an error message. For example:

buffer (stale after 1 hours)

1. Create a new section in the DLE of the 'inc qvd' app and add the following code:

(see data sources\qvd\buffer example.txt)

test_buffer:

buffer (stale after 1 hours)

LOAD @1

FROM

'lib://qvd data/testbuffer.txt'

(txt, codepage is 1252, no labels, delimiter is '\t', msq);

2. The output will be:

test_buffer << testbuffer

Lines fetched: 1

3. Reload the app and you will see that a qvd file with a long filename such as the one below has been created in the buffer location:

04b836a11d19bbcfda8103e227a38d36b8a575ac.qvd

4. You will be able to find the buffer in the following location:

C:\Users\<username>\Documents\Qlik\Sense\Buffers

Where <username> is the username you are logged on to the machine as.

Completed App:

Advanced\QVDs\inc qvd-buffers.qvf

QVD OPTIMIZATION

The reason for checking that the qvd load is optimized is that it means you will get a faster load of your data.

You can check if the qvd load is optimized by looking in the script execution progress for the text '(qvd optimized)'.

If your table of data is large enough you will probably notice in the time taken to reload the app that optimized.

Your QVD load will not be optimized if there are transformations (such as functions) or filtering except EXISTS in WHERE clause.

USEFUL QVD FUNCTIONS

QVD and File functions

There are several file functions that can be used to get extra information on files.

We will cover some of the more useful ones next:

The FOR EACH loop can be used in conjunction with the filelist command to loop around a list of files.

Filelist(path_to_files)

path_to_files - this is the path to the files to process and can be a string or variable.

This example will process all the qvd files in the folder c:\myfolder:

FOR EACH *vFileName* in filelist('c:\myfolder\' & '*.qvd')

....some commands...

NEXT;

Filelist example

1. In the 'inc qvd' app, go to the DLE and create a section called 'QVD Functions'.

2. Add the following code to the new section:

(see file data sources\qvd\qvd status.txt)

LET *Last_Updated* = today();

FOR EACH *FileName* in filelist('c:*.qvd')

QVDStatus:

LOAD

'$(Last_Updated)' as QVD_last_updated,

Date(QvdCreateTime('$(FileName)') ,'YYYY-MM-DD hh:mm:ss') as FileTimeStamp,

QvdNoOfRecords('$(FileName)') as QVD_record_count,

QvdTableName('$(FileName)') as QVD_table

AUTOGENERATE 1;

NEXT;

3. Reload the app. Go to the DMV and check the data in the QVDStatus table.

CREATE QVDS FOR EACH TABLE IN AN EXISTING APP

Sometimes you might want to create QVDs for a Qlik Sense app that you have already developed.

1. Open the 'inc qvd' app and go to the DLE.

2. Create a section called 'QVD Loop' and make sure it is the last section.

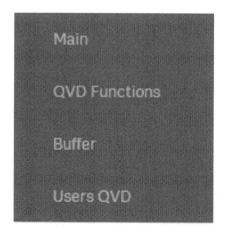

≡ **QVD Loop**

3. Add the following code to the 'QVD Loop' section:

(see file: data sources\qvd\qvd loop.txt)

```
//STORE TABLES AS QVD
SET vDataDir = 'QVD\';
for i=0 to NoOfTables()-1
LET d= TableName(i);
STORE $(d) into $(vDataDir)\$(d).QVD;
NEXT
LET j = NoOfTables();
do while j > 0
let d = TableName(0);
drop table $(d);
```

let j = NoOfTables();

loop

Completed App:

Advanced\QVDs\inc qvd-qvd loop.qvf

4. Create a folder called QVD in the same folder as your 'inc qvd.qvf' file. The QVD folder will be used to store your QVDs.

5. The code loops around all the tables using the for loop:

for <initial number> to <last number>

...some commands...

Next

6. For each table it gets the name using the TableName function and then uses the STORE command to create a qvd.

7. Finally a while loop is used to drop the tables. This part of the code is optional and will mean that the data is removed from the app.

The format of the while loop is:

do while <some condition>

...<some commands>...

Loop

8. One difference between the for and while loops is that the for loop will run for a limited number of files whereas the while loop has the potential to run forever if the condition is never met ie: 1=0.

SUMMARY

Creating qvds in the most efficient manner possible is an important technique to learn if you intend to develop qlik sense apps in a working environment.

Creating QVDs also means that data can easily be shared between qlik sense apps if required and only read from the data source the once.

One useful tool for viewing the contents of a qvd quickly is called qviewer the url to try this tool is http://easyqlik.com/.

QLIK SENSE EXTENSIONS

Extensions can add some great features to your QlikView document.

For example you can display calendars, other web pages and integrate your Qlik Sense app with google maps.

For a good introduction to Javascript visit http://w3schools.com.

1. Go to this folder:

C:\Users\<username>\Documents\Qlik\Examples\Extensions

2. Copy the folder HelloWorld to the following folder:

C:\Users\<username>\Documents\Qlik\Sense\Extensions

3. Open the Qlik Sense desktop and create an new app called 'extensions'

4. Create a new sheet called 'my extensions', open and edit the sheet.

5. Notice that in the left hand pane you have an object called 'Hello World':

6. Drag and drop the 'Hello World' object to the sheet to create the extension.

7. The 'Hello World' simply prints the text 'Hello World !" on your sheet.

EXTENSION FILES

The Hello World extension consists of 3 files:

1. Javascript file: com-qliktech-helloworld.js

This file consists of the javascript to display the extension.

2. QEXT File : com-qliktech-helloworld.qext

The .qext file consists on a description of the extension including information such as:

- name
- description
- preview - This is the preview image, in this case helloworld.png
- type - visualization
- version
- author

3. Image: helloworld.png

This is the image that is used as a preview when you right click on the extension object when selecting from the charts tab.

WEBSITE EXTENSION

1. Copy the folder MyExtension from the 'Advanced\ Extensions' in the sample data to your Extensions folder:

C:\Users\<username>\Documents\Qlik\Sense\ Extensions

2. Open the extension file: myextension.js in the

MyExtension folder.

This extension simply displays a website using the following iframe html:

<iframe src='http://www.techstuffy.com' width='100%' height='100%'>test</iframe>

3. Open the 'extensions' app you have created or create a new app and add the 'My Extension' extension to a new sheet.

4. Right click on the My Extension object to see the preview image:

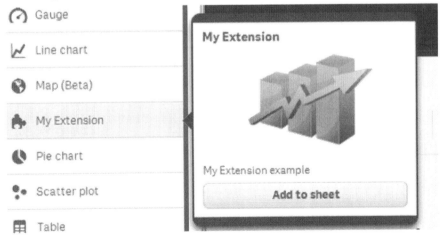

5. Click Done and Save.

6. Try changing the website from www.techstuffy.com to another, press F5 to refresh the screen.

7. Finally try exploring code by right clicking on the extension and selecting either 'dev tools' or 'view source'.

Hopefully you can see that even with simple html you can create interesting extensions to add to your apps.

To get more information on Extensions go to:

http://branch.qlik.com

http://community.qlik.com/community/new-to-qlik-sense

(see w3schools.com for more information on html and javascript)

PART 7. FURTHER

WHAT NEXT?

"Knowledge isn't power until it is applied." – Dale Carnegie

Working your way through this book is only the beginning of your Qlik learning.

The best way to continue to learn qlik sense is to think of projects that might be useful to yourself.

I personally started to learn QlikView by developing documents to track my spending habits and monitor aspects of Microsoft SQL servers.

You will really start to learn what you can do with Qlik Sense when you start to develop apps for other people and they start to ask the 'Can it do XYZ?'.

Using the Qlik Sense server (if available) you will be able to share your apps with other users and hopefully you will be able to start using Qlik Sense within your company.

Some other good news is that most of the scripting language you used in the DLE can also be applied to QlikView documents as well as Qlik Sense apps.

This will be useful when using qlik within a company where you might have to maintain qlikview and qlik sense apps.

THANK YOU

I'd like to say "thank you" for purchasing my guide.

If you liked what you've read then please take a moment to leave a review for this book on Amazon.

The feedback will help me write the books that will help you get results.

If you have any questions please contact me using the contact page at www.techstuffy.com.

Good luck with all your future qliking.

Mark

TechStuffy Books - Amazon Author Page:

www.techstuffybooks.com

APPENDIX

USEFUL WEBSITES

These are some websites I recommend:

Qlik sites

http://qlik.com

http://community.qlikview.com

Obvious first source of information for Qlik Sense and a great community of users.

http://techstuffy.com

The site for this book and other information about qlikview and SQL server.

http://techstuffybooks.com

For more details for books published by techstuffy.

Any corrections and downloads available that can be used with this book will be on this site.

SQL Server sites

http://Microsoft.com/SQLserver

http://SQLservercentral.com

Web Development

http://w3schools.com

For learning various programming languages such as javascript and html which it useful for Qlik Sense Extension development.

INDEX

A

B

C

D

E

G

Printed in Great Britain
by Amazon